Fullness of Joy

The Many Faces of Joy in the Christian Life

BRUCE MARTIN

FULLNESS OF JOY: The Many Faces of Joy in the Christian Life
Copyright 2023

College Press Publishing
417-623-6280, collegepress.com

ISBN: 978-0-89900-988-9 (paperback)
ISBN: 978-0-89900-989-6 (eBook)

Dedicated to
Judy

my lovely wife of over fifty years,

who has always been there for me,

and who has greatly contributed to making

our lives a wonderful adventure.

TABLE OF CONTENTS

PREFACE

The theme of "joy" has been prevalent in American society for a long time. An emphasis on finding and having joy swirls all around us. It surfaces constantly in the realm of advertising and marketing. The candy bar "Almond Joy" has been with us since 1946, and the dishwashing liquid "Joy" has been available since 1949. These names were not chosen by accident. Munching on an Almond Joy is intended to bring joy to your taste buds, and washing dishes with Joy will, hopefully, make everything sparkle resulting in joy.

In recent years, "joy marketing" actually became an advertising buzzword as a vast array of companies chose "joy" as part of their approach in appealing to the public. Including "joy" in a marketing campaign is intended to bring out very positive feelings and emotions. A national pizza chain supposedly "owns the emotional territory of joy." In the real estate world, there is the "joy of that new home feeling." In banking, you can experience "moments of joy" or the "joy of digital banking." An arthritis cream promises the "joy of movement," and a dessert topping comes with "the sound of joy" when you press the nozzle on its container and spread its' contents over your pie or cobbler (more examples to follow in chapter one).

This emphasis on joy pops up in all kinds of everyday experiences. Friends might return from a Caribbean cruise and say that "it was a real joy."

You might go to a family gathering and declare "it was such a joy to see everyone again," especially if it had been a while since being together. Of course, new parents return home from the hospital with "a bundle of joy." A person might relay that the vintage car they have worked long and hard to restore is their "pride and joy." A high school senior might "jump for joy" upon receiving an acceptance letter from the college/university that was their first choice. Some have even been known to shed "tears of joy" because of being overcome by some happy, uplifting moment (I recently heard that a major league baseball player cried when told he was selected to be on the All-Star Team). Anything that occasions joy is always welcome and highly sought after.

What is proposed in the following pages is that all of these examples and many others from everyday life constitute a "general" form of joy. There is, however, a higher level of joy that is only available to us in the spiritual realm, through God, Christ, and the Holy Spirit. This higher level of joy is what the Scriptures refer to as "fullness of joy" or "complete joy." General joy comes about because of good happenings and pleasant circumstances. Fullness, complete, or ultimate joy depends solely on being grounded in God. This kind of joy can be present even amidst trying circumstances.

The world of "fullness of joy" is what we plan to explore in the chapters of this book. I hope you will join me for the journey. Ultimately, I hope you will come to experience joy as God intends for us to experience it, i.e., constantly, even in the midst of circumstances that you may have thought were highly unlikely or "off-limits" to joy. Life on this higher level is what God desires for us all.

THE FULLNESS OF JOY

"In Your presence is fullness of joy. . .".
Psalm 16:11b (NKJV)

It was the first trip to the ocean for our two young children. From our landlocked home in Indiana, the Navy was sending us to San Diego for my first tour as a chaplain, and the four of us were ready to take in the majesty of the Pacific after our first day in town. I will always remember the reaction of our daughter. Christine loves the water and, upon seeing the ocean and changing into her swimsuit, she plunged in and jumped and swam and played until she was worn out. Delight was written all over her face. It was an exhilarating time of pure, innocent joy for an eight-year old.

Our son, on the other hand, didn't have the same response. James liked the sand and the beach, but that was as far as he wanted to venture. Those previous swimming lessons hadn't been all to his liking. Getting water in his face and diving under water wasn't his thing. He could take or leave a backyard wadding pool; what would he want with a vast expanse of open sea? His joy came from a well-timed swing launching a plastic baseball over the front yard fence, then watching his dad stumble over the fence to retrieve it. For him, at age six, nothing was more exciting, not even his first experience with the ocean.

Joy comes in many packages; it has many faces. "Delight" and "gladness" are some of the words we use to describe it, along with others such as "exhilaration," "exuberance," and "elation." However, it also comes in less intense forms. It may refer to an inner, abiding peace and calm, based on a sense of security and confidence in God and our Lord Jesus Christ. In this regard, it can be present no matter what may be taking place in our lives.

With these thoughts in mind, we might say that there is both a "general joy" and an "ultimate joy" that can be known. The "general" type is what society at large talks about and hopes to encounter on a regular basis. This is what Christine and James were experiencing in seeing the ocean and hitting a ball. It happens, hopefully, on special occasions such as weddings, birthdays, anniversaries, and graduations. For a while, a leading toy retailer claimed to be "The Joy Store," with joy (supposedly) the assured result from shopping and spending money on the premises, then playing with whatever game, action figure, doll, train set, etc., had been selected. It occurs when a baseball team that hasn't won the World Series in generations miraculously breaks through to become World Champions, allowing its' long-suffering fans to proclaim that they can now die in peace (witness the Boston Red Sox and Chicago Cubs of fairly recent vintage). Joy might strike after going to H & R Block and discovering that a tax return is in order instead of taxes still being owed. It presumably occurs with food. Over the years, while browsing in bookstores or surfing the Internet, I have come across books on *The Joy of Blueberries, The Joy of Cranberries,* and *The Joy of Rhubarb* (who knew). Of course, *The Joy of Cooking* has been a popular seller for a long, long time. Certainly, joy in the general sense of finding delight and gladness in our daily lives comes from many sources.

The "ultimate" type of joy comes from only one source – God. The full text of the verse mentioned to introduce this chapter states: "You will show me the path of life; In Your presence is fullness of joy; At Your right hand are pleasures for evermore" (Psalm 16:11, NKJV). Other verses speak of this idea of "full" or "complete" joy in the Lord as well. In John 15, after speaking of Himself as the "true vine" and encouraging us to abide in Him, Jesus said, "I have told you this so that my joy may be in you and that your joy may be complete" (vs. 11, see also John 17:13). Obviously, Christ is saying that a direct correlation exists between abiding, being spiritually grounded in His will and ways, and knowing joy that is complete. John continues this theme in 1 John 1:4 where he writes, "We write this to make our joy complete." In this instance, complete joy is associated with knowing who Jesus Christ is, proclaiming Him, and having fellowship with Him (see the first three verses of this chapter).

The message of these passages is that any fullness of joy is related to matters of faith; ultimate joy doesn't come from the "happy" things of life but the spiritual and a relationship with the One who made us and oversees all things. Thus, this ultimate, full, complete joy can still be present even though we have nagging bills, but Publisher's Clearing House hasn't yet knocked on our door to make us a million-dollar winner, because God takes care of His own. It can still be present even though we may have been overlooked for that promotion at work since God and Christ are always there to remind us of our overall worth and value, and of what truly matters in life. It can still be present even though we face a debilitating, perhaps life-threatening illness, because our Lord provides all needed strength and reassurance, and extends promises that are valid both in life and in death. It comes down to this – joy in the Lord, fullness of joy, generates a confidence in our ability, through Him, to ultimately triumph and overcome in life that cannot be displaced by the circumstances and demands that swirl around us. It is a "state of delight and well-being that results from knowing and serving God."[1]

This is not to say that this confidence cannot be battered. In Matthew 7:24-27, Jesus spoke of the wise and foolish persons, the former who elected to build a house on rock while the latter proceeded to build a house on sand. In both cases, rain and floods and winds came that beat upon the two dwellings; however, the aftermath of the storms was entirely different. The house on the rock "did not fall," but the house on the sand had structural/foundation problems and did fall. In fact, "it fell with a great crash." Consequently, building a house on rock, on the solid foundation of faith in God and our Lord Jesus Christ, does not mean that our lives will be off limits to storms, to "high winds and heavy seas" (to quote a good Navy term). What it does mean is that the person of faith has the means to survive the storms and not be washed away in the rain, floods, and winds. Like Israel of old in the midst of trials, "If the LORD had not been on our side. . . the flood would have engulfed us, the torrent would have swept over us, the raging waters would have swept us away" (Psalm 124:1, 4-5). The fact that we do not get swept away lifts us up, sustains us, and prompts us to rejoice and praise God.

So why would we want to look into this matter of joy, specifically "ultimate" or "fullness of joy"? Why would it be worthwhile to devote an entire book to this particular theme? The reasons, I believe, number three: 1) it is a recurring theme in Scripture that God deems as significant and essential; 2) it is sometimes overlooked and/or undermined as an important component of the Christian life; and 3) it pops up in some surprising places that we do not typically associate with the possibility of joy. Let's take a few minutes to examine these three thoughts.

First of all, joy is a recurring theme throughout the Bible as the following indicates:

---

1. Chad Brand and Eric Alan Mitchell, eds., *Holman Illustrated Bible Dictionary* (Nashville: B&H Publishing Group, 2015), 934.

A number of Greek and Hebrew words are used to convey the ideas of joy and rejoicing. We have the same situation in English with such nearly synonymous words as joy, happiness, pleasure, delight, gladness, merriment, felicity, and enjoyment. The words "joy" and "rejoice" are the words used most often to translate the Hebrew and Greek words into English. Joy is found over 150 times in the Bible. If such words as "joyous" and "joyful" are included, the number comes to over 200. The verb "rejoice" appears over 200 times.[2]

Here is a general sampling of the many references to joy/rejoice in Scripture:

Nehemiah 8:10 – "Nehemiah said, 'Go and enjoy choice food and sweet drinks and send some to those who have nothing prepared. This day is sacred to our LORD. Do not grieve, for the joy of the LORD is your strength.'"

Psalm 43:3-4 – "Send forth your light and your truth, let them guide me; let them bring me to your holy mountain, to the place where your dwell. Then I will go to the altar of God, to God, my joy and my delight. I will praise you with the harp, O God, my God."

Psalm 92:4 – "For you make me glad by your deeds, O LORD; I sing for joy at the works of your hands."

Psalm 119:111 – "Your statutes are my heritage forever; they are the joy of my heart."

Proverbs 12:20 – "There is deceit in the hearts of those who plot evil, but joy for those who promote peace."

Isaiah 51:11 – "The ransomed of the LORD will return.

They will enter Zion with singing; everlasting joy will crown their heads. Gladness and joy will overtake them, and sorrow and sighing will flee away."

Matthew 13:44 – "The kingdom of heaven is like treasure hidden in a field. When a man found it, he hid it again, and then in his joy went and sold all he had and bought that field."

Romans 14:17 – "For the kingdom of God is not a matter of eating and drinking, but of righteousness, peace and joy in the Holy Spirit. . .".

Romans 15:13 – "May the God of hope fill you with all joy and peace as you trust in him, so that you may overflow with hope by the power of the Holy Spirit."

Galatians 5:22 – "But the fruit of the Spirit is love, joy, peace, patience, kindness, goodness, faithfulness, gentleness and self-control. Against such things there is no law."

Philippians 1:25-26 – "Convinced of this, I know that I will remain, and I will continue with all of you for your progress and joy in the faith, so that through my being with you again your joy in Christ Jesus will overflow on account of me."

Philippians 4:4 – "Rejoice in the Lord always. I will say it again: Rejoice!"

1 Thessalonians 5:16-18 – "Be joyful always; pray continually; give thanks in all circumstances, for this is God's will for you in Christ Jesus."

Hebrews 12:1-2 – "Therefore, since we are surrounded by such a great cloud of witnesses, let us throw off everything that hinders and the sin that so easily entangles, and let us run with perseverance the race marked out for us. Let us fix our eyes on Jesus, the author and perfecter of our faith, who for the joy set before him endured the cross, scorning its shame, and sat down at the right hand of the throne of God."

With just this sampling, it is obvious that joy and rejoicing are intended to be a vital part of our spiritual lives. Along with prayer and gratitude in the 1 Thess. 5 passage, it is a constant element of our walk with the Lord and a product of life in the Holy Spirit (Gal. 5). It is not something we are meant to experience infrequently, only when we get around to it after dealing with everything else in our lives. Instead, God's plan is for joy to permeate, to continually invade our thinking and our living.

Another good reason for looking at this theme seriously is because we may overlook the significant place of joy in the Christian life, especially since it is often undermined in the ebb and flow of our daily pursuits. America is certainly the land of opportunity where what we become and where we end up does not depend on our social standing at birth, our ethnicity, our religious background, etc. However, the other side of this can be – as we seek to achieve and advance and become – that we spend much of our lives striving and competing for items such as grades, awards, jobs, responsibilities in order that we may excel and be noticed, receive raises and promotions, perhaps even vie for affection.

A *Dilbert* cartoon once showed the boss counseling Alice, one of the female colleagues. The discussion unfolded as follows: 1st frame – "Here are your regular goals and here are your stretch goals"; 2nd frame – "What's the difference?"; 3rd frame – "The regular goals can be achieved by sacrificing your health and your personal life"; 4th frame – "The stretch goals require all of that plus some sort of criminal conduct." After a couple of other inane remarks, the session concludes as the boss says, "Maybe we should talk about the ultra-stretchy goals later." I would like to think that these remarks express exaggeration, but many probably feel that this isn't far from reality.

Additionally, a great deal of life can be spent trying to fit in (a reality that is not the domain of teenagers alone). Or, much of life can be spent balancing hectic schedules and being concerned about our health, our children and loved ones, our finances, and our future. An editorial page cartoon was on target when it showed a patient in bed talking to his doctor. Across the top was written, "Researchers investigate why Americans don't get enough sleep." In the caption, the patient says, "Three jobs is a long day. That only leaves 5 ½ hours for uninterrupted worrying about my debts and no health insurance." So, who has time for joy when we are interacting with such realities (or near realities) as this? We can understand that it might crop up every now and then, but to expect joy to be an ongoing, continuing part of such lives seems to lean rather heavily in the direction of wishful thinking.

And even when it does come, joy can be mixed with and offset by other events. Several years ago, I went to the mailbox and found two letters from my churches' publishing house. The first letter contained a check for an article I had submitted and had, subsequently, been included in the weekly publication (now monthly) that goes out to all of our churches. This called for joy, the combination of the check and the fact that the piece had been accepted and published. The other letter wasn't very uplifting. It concerned another article I had written and submitted, and they were writing to inform me that the material "did not meet their publishing needs at this time," the time-honored way of telling you that they didn't want the result of your brilliant thought and hard work. So, what are you supposed to do with such opposing messages? At least, I didn't use the check in some stupid way to numb my disappointment.

On another occasion, while stationed at the Naval Air Station, Sigonella, Sicily, I had an extremely busy day ahead of me. Along with the family, I was scheduled to head north the following day for a chaplain's conference and retreat in Germany. I had lots to do to wrap everything up before leaving. On this particular day, I served as a member of a panel discussion group, did a couple of counseling sessions, wrote an annual evaluation for one of our Religious Program Specialists (Chaplain's Assistant), along with several other odds and ends. I was feeling a good sense of satisfaction over getting it all done and being in good shape to leave, a measure of joy if you please, and then it happened. The base at Sigonella has two main areas that are about eight miles apart, one area containing the support facilities (e.g., schools, commissary, housing, chapel, etc.) and the other containing the airfield and operational side of the base. In going back and forth between the two, I was in a little bit of a hurry that day and passed several cars on the road.

Shortly after arriving back at my office, I received a phone call from the Executive Officer, the second in command on the base. He was calling to inform me that, in my haste, I had passed the Commanding Officer's car and the CO would like for me to observe more caution in the future. Thus, on a day when I thought I should have received a commendation for all of my frantic efforts, what I received instead was a very unwanted, less than positive phone call from my superiors. Indeed, joy can be mixed with and offset by other events that can cloud our experience unless we are in tune with the ultimate kind of joy.

It is also noteworthy that, in the Scriptures, joy shows up in some surprising, unexpected places. For Christ, as evident in Hebrews 12:1-2, it was somehow involved in the Calvary experience as He looked beyond the immediate suffering and darkness to the eternal good for humankind that would result from the excruciatingly painful ordeal of the Cross. And for all of us, times of trials in our lives are not to be occasions for lapsing into self-pity and complaining. Instead, according to James (see 1:2-4), they can be tempered with joy due to the spiritual benefits that can result, e.g., enhancing character; drawing us closer to the Lord whereby we experience more of God's help, nearness, and grace; and equipping us to better understand and minister to others in need (more on this later). Surely, this doesn't mean that trials should be viewed through the lens of joy rather than the lens of inconvenience, disdain, or disgust? Unless I'm reading James incorrectly, surely it does. Of course, at this point, we're obviously talking about the lens of ultimate joy, not the lens of general joy.

There is one more surprising place where ultimate joy does not desert us – in death. This is not to overlook the fact that other emotions and feelings are involved when death comes knocking, and we face the earthly loss of a loved one or our own final moments in this life. Even Christians grieve at such times; however, our faith and the promises of the Lord make it possible so that we do not grieve as others "who have no hope" (1 Thess. 4:13). A long time ago, the Psalmist told us, "Precious in the sight of the LORD is the death of his saints" (i.e., "faithful ones," Ps. 116:15). Our departure and that of our loved ones, when anchored in the Lord, is merely a passage into the eternal presence of God where "He will wipe every tear from their eyes. There will be no more death or mourning or crying or pain, for the old order of things has passed away" (Rev. 21:4). With this perspective, ultimate joy remains intact even in death for, then, it becomes a beginning, not an ending, for the child of God is simply ushered into the glories of eternal life with the Savior. Even here, our confidence in our ability to triumph and overcome through Him is not displaced.

Let us, then, undertake this journey of discovering the true place and significance of joy, specifically the ultimate kind in the Christian life. Our goal will be to uncover and live in its fullness, realizing that God does not intend for it to be a matter that only surfaces occasionally and temporarily, but an inner quality that always sustains us and permeates our existence. My prayer is that the chapters that follow – dealing with such themes as joy and God, Christ and salvation, forgiveness, worship, and others – will help to open up new dimensions in our walk of faith. Enjoy!

THE JOY OF GOD

"Then I will go to the altar of God,
To God my exceeding joy. . .".

Psalm 43:4a (NKJV)

During my several decades of life, there are numerous things I have learned that it is best not to do. Here are a few examples of my "keen" powers of observation:

— Don't wave to a child who is learning to ride a bike. Inevitably, the youngster wants to please you by waving back and the results can be disastrous.

— Don't walk down an icy, sloping driveway with your hands in your pockets while going out to retrieve the paper on a winter morning. It took me two episodes to learn this lesson. Yes, it should have only taken one (or none).

— Don't back out of your driveway at 6 a.m. and, because it's dark and hardly anyone is stirring, assume no one is behind you. You guessed it, there's a story here, but surely it was my fellow carpooler who got his wires

21

crossed, not me, and was off a day on whose turn it was to drive.

— If you've been inactive through the winter and start to play softball in the spring, don't run the bases full tilt the first time out of the batter's box. Easing back into things may not be very "macho," but it helps to avoid those pulled muscles and being forced to watch two or three games from the dugout until you recover.

These may be fairly minor lessons learned but the biggest lesson of all is this: <u>Don't try to live life without God</u>. Why? Not only is He the creator and sustainer of all that is, the fountain-head of true wisdom and the One who knows best how to live life, the source of salvation, and the ground of meaning and purpose, but God is also the source of ultimate, full, and complete joy.

Depending on how we were raised and our experiences over the years, joy may not be the first thought that comes to mind when we think of God. Fear may be a candidate for our initial response if themes such as hell, judgment, and guilt have been prominent in our faith journey. Apathy and indifference may raise their heads if our exposure to matters of faith has been somewhat limited or if we view the spiritual life as merely an option that some people are attracted to, not as an essential element for all of us to incorporate into our lives. Resentment may even be involved if we have had some kind of negative experience with a church or with religious people who weren't all that we thought they should be, or if we feel that life has treated us unfairly and God should have done something to make things turn out better. It may be necessary to grapple with some of these thoughts and feelings as we interact with the ups and downs of life. However, I believe that we can live on a higher, more positive level of life if our primary response to the mention of God is JOY!

One definition of "exceeding" is "to be greater than or superior to." Thus, the Psalmist is telling us that if we are interested in the greatest joy, in superior joy, our search needs to carry us to God. Landing anywhere else and settling for what it might offer will only result in some inferior, lower grade of joy. If you collect sports cards and have your choice of some different possibilities, would you choose something in "fair" or "good" condition when a card in "mint" condition is also available? If someone offered to take you anywhere in town for dinner, would you swing by the local root beer and hot dog stand or opt for the five-star restaurant that serves fine steaks and seafood that you've always wanted to try? There's nothing wrong with root beer and hot dogs but given the choice – come on now! Or, if you are stepping out for an important, dress-up event and could have your hair styled by your untrained neighbor or by "the stylist to the stars," who would you choose? So, if you can have some joy or exceeding joy, what is the logical choice? The logical choice is – *God.*

How is it, then, that God is the source of exceeding joy in our lives? For me, I think this is realized when we live and bask in several basic realities about God. Others might have some additional thoughts, but the joy of God can certainly be linked to such realities as the following:

God's track record of faithfulness is unblemished. Perhaps Joshua said it best when he stated, "Now I am about to go the way of all the earth. You know with all your heart and soul that not one of all the good promises the LORD your God gave you has failed. Every promise has been fulfilled; not one has failed" (Joshua 23:14).

This is a pretty big claim, that not one of God's promises to the Israelites had ever failed. All of the promises involving deliverance from Egypt, provision in the wilderness, moving into the promised land, and God's presence and guidance through it all had never missed a beat. No doubt, all of these things did not occur according to the timetable the Israelites may have preferred. If they had taken a vote, they probably would have skipped that forty years of wandering around in the desert stuff, but God was true and all the promises were fulfilled in His good time.

And, for Joshua personally, I find this statement particularly interesting in light of what God had promised to him in chapter one, verse five: "No one will be able to stand up against you all the days of your life. As I was with Moses, so I will be with you; I will never leave you or forsake you." If I was taking over for one of the central figures in all of the Old Testament, I think I might experience a fair amount of anxiety. Moses had led God's people through the major defining period in the entire history of Israel. Moses had been God's instrument of power and wisdom and deliverance. God had sustained him through gaining the people's confidence; through interacting with a deceitful, "promise one thing, do something else later" Pharaoh; through leading the Israelites out of Egypt (the weak overcoming the mighty); through wandering in the wilderness for forty years; and through dealing with an incomprehensible array of complaints, ingratitude, and lapses in faith on the part of the people. Moses was a legend, destined to appear later with Christ on the Mount of Transfiguration, and now Joshua must step into his shoes. God's promise was that He would be with Joshua in the same powerful way. And, after the years had passed on another hectic and significant period in the life of Israel, Joshua testified that not one promise had ever failed!

God's record of faithfulness is still intact today. Sometimes, usually out of misunderstanding or unrealistic expectations, we may question whether or not God's record here is truly unblemished. It seems, at times, that God should have done more to help, that He held back when jumping in would have alleviated our problems, that He should have supported us more in line with what we had in mind. However, when we impose our wishes and expectations onto what God should be doing, it often leads to making up promises never mentioned in the Scriptures.

The "Big Three" of biblical promises since the coming of Christ are these: 1) the forgiveness of sins through the sacrifice of the Savior; 2) the indwelling presence of the Holy Spirit equipping Christians for a fulfilling, empowering, and, ultimately, victorious life in this world; and 3) eternal life for the child of God when this earthly life has run its course. Under number two, there are certainly promises for help and strength to successfully manage whatever turns life may take, whether they be to our liking or not to our liking. But, there is no promise of a stress-free, problem-free life, even for God's people (remember the wise and foolish builders and the "equal opportunity" rain, floods, and winds). *We live with human natures in a fallen world with self- interest rife all around us.* If that isn't a formula for struggles, problems, challenges, and bad things popping up for decent people, I don't know what is. If we believe that the Christian is immune to any kind of serious irritation or difficulty, then somehow we have made up, imagined, or assumed promises that are not really there.

As the people of God today, traveling through the wilderness of life, our experience is the same as Joshua's and the children of Israel. We can be sure that not one promise for strengthening us, sustaining us, seeing us through, and saving us will ever fail. And, in this, there is great and exceeding joy.

Here's another reality, closely related to the above, that speaks to the exceeding joy of God: *Grounded in God and Christ, we are never in over our heads in the situations of life.* The Scriptures refer to his reality in such passages as the following:

> He who dwells in the shelter of the Most High will rest in the shadow of the Almighty. I will say of the LORD, "He is my refuge and my fortress, my God, in whom I trust." Surely he will save you from the fowler's snare and from

25

the deadly pestilence. He will cover you with his feathers, and under his wings you will find refuge; his faithfulness will be your shield and rampart (Psalm 91:1-4).

Those who trust in the LORD are like Mount Zion, which cannot be shaken, but endures forever. As the mountains surround Jerusalem, so the LORD surrounds his people both now and forevermore (Psalm 125:1-2).

When you pass through the waters, I will be with you: and when you pass through the rivers, they will not sweep over you. When you walk through the fire, you will not be burned; the flames will not set you ablaze. For I am the LORD, your God, the Holy One of Israel, your Savior. . . (Isaiah 43:2-3a).

Come to me, all you who are weary and burdened, and I will give you rest (Matthew 11:28).

No temptation has seized you except what is common to man. And God is faithful; he will not let you be tempted beyond what you can bear. But when you are tempted, he will also provide a way out so that you can stand up under it (1 Corinthians 10:13).

I can do everything through him who gives me strength (Philippians 4:13).

Some of these Old Testament passages apply to specific situations for Israel of old, but they still appear to be relevant to God's people today. We will talk more later about a couple of these wonderful promises.

What all of this means is that we are never left alone and that we have help and resources beyond our own human help and resources. What it means is that we are never in over our heads as we confront and manage the twists and turns of life because of the presence of God.

If we lack the means and the resources for handling a situation, we can be overwhelmed as we face a grim outcome. However, if sufficient means and resources are available, we forge ahead even though the situation may present a challenge and require some effort on our part. If a farmer has several hundred acres of ground to prepare and only has a horse with a pull-behind plow, he or she may lapse into despair. But, if the farmer has the latest John Deere equipment (and a tractor cab with air-conditioning and surround-sound stereo to boot!), the job becomes manageable and its threatening aspects fade away. Or, if I'm headed to Europe and (for some strange reason) only have a rowboat to cross the ocean, panic quickly takes over my every waking thought (and maybe my dreams, too!). But, if I have a berth on a luxury cruise liner, panic is replaced by confidence and anticipation of what is to come.

So, for us in the swirl of life, panic and despair need not take over our thoughts since we always have the means and resources we need to manage our circumstances in the presence and power of God. There may be challenges, but God has promised to be with us and to add His divine help and resources to our own. Even if the challenge becomes life-threatening, as with certain illnesses, we know that God is still there to care for us, first in this life and then in the life to come.

My first assignment as a Navy chaplain in San Diego was aboard an amphibious landing ship, the USS VANCOUVER (LPD-2). After about eight months onboard, the ship left for a six-month Western Pacific (WESTPAC) deployment that put us on station in the Indian Ocean during the Iranian hostage situation in the early 1980s. I had a Chaplain's Bulletin Board in one of the main passageways, so I gathered up some inspirational posters to display during the months we were gone. I remember one of the posters very vividly. It showed a polar bear cub romping over some rocks and had this caption: "Help me to remember, Lord, that nothing is going to happen today that you and me can't handle together." That was a great, uplifting and encouraging thought for 800 Sailors and Marines who were far from home in a very uncertain environment. It remains a great, uplifting and encouraging thought today and reminds us of the exceeding joy that we can know in God.

For me, *the overwhelming reality that the most powerful being in the universe constantly thinks about me, cares for me, and wants to see good things happen for me* also accounts for exceeding joy in my relationship with God.

Here again, we may sometimes wonder about this reality since each one of us is such a small part of this world and the vast human family. Our daughter now lives in New York City and on one of our visits we did the Empire State Building scene. Looking out over that great fascinating city and straining to see the specks that were people down below, I pondered whether or not God knew where I was and what I was doing. Or, walking through Time's Square with its masses of people, I tend to get philosophical and wonder if God can really be a personal God who knows who I am in the midst of all this activity and humanity. However, the Scriptures (and my experience) reaffirm that God is a personal God who is there to care, provide, and guide.

Psalm 139 talks about how we are "fearfully and wonderfully made" and that God knew us even before we were born (vss. 14-16). The passage goes on to state: "How precious to me are your thoughts, O God! How vast is the sum of them! Were I to count them, they would outnumber the grains of sand" (vss. 17-18). Another reading of this is "how precious *concerning* me are your thoughts." If we want to get some idea of how much we are in God's thoughts, we could go out and count grains of sand on the seashores around the world and, when we were done, we could declare that His thoughts toward us are more numerous than the humongous number that would result.

However, since no one among us has the time, inclination, or the patience to do this, we merely conclude that it is unfathomable how much God thinks about us. How does God do it? I have no idea. I am clueless. I just stand in awe and rejoice!

And, as God thinks about us, He desires to provide for us and see good things come to pass in our lives. The Scriptures talk about this in such passages as Matthew 6 and 7. The familiar words of Matthew 6:25-34 remind us that God lovingly provides for the birds of the air – "they do not sow or reap or store away in barns, and yet your heavenly Father feeds them" (vs. 26). Here's the kicker, "Are you not more valuable than they?" No need to think twice, the answer is a resounding "yes." If God provides for the creatures of creation, do you think He is going to neglect the crowning touch of creation, i.e., you and me! Certainly not. If we "seek first his kingdom and his righteousness," then the things needed for the living of life will be provided.

Matthew 7 adds to this picture. In the verses about asking, seeking, and knocking (7-11), Jesus said: "If you, then, though you are evil, know how to give good gifts to your children, how much more will your Father in heaven give good gifts to those who ask him!" In other words, if we, who are saddled with human natures and moments of moodiness, impatience, and irritability as we function as parents, still know how to give good gifts to our children, what do you think we can expect of God as the divine Parent of us all? We can expect His goodness to be in play in all that He does.

How vast is the number of God's thoughts toward us, *how much more valuable* are we in God's eyes than the creatures of this world, and *how much more* will the Father give good things to those who ask – these are truly overwhelming thoughts about God that lead to exceeding joy.

There is at least one more reality about God that accounts for exceeding joy, viz., *the wonder of His invitation and the wonder of His mercy.*

Have you ever *really* stopped to think about what God invites us to and desires to share with us? In the Parable of the Wedding Banquet, we see that "the kingdom of heaven is like a king [God] who prepared a wedding banquet for his son" (Matthew 22:1). In the Parable of the Great Banquet, we learn that "a certain man [God] was preparing a great banquet and invited many guests" (Luke 14:16). And, in the Parable of the Prodigal Son, when the prodigal returned, the father's [God's] first inclination was to have a feast and to celebrate (Luke 15:23-24). It turns out that God is the Great Caterer and Party Host. He likes banquets and feasts. He likes celebrating and festive occasions. And, when He invites us into fellowship, the invitation is to come and share in the joyous Banquet that He has prepared.

Unfortunately, as the first two parables just mentioned unfold, many refuse the invitation, either ignoring it or making excuses or even becoming hostile over it. All of this is hard to understand given the nature of the invitation. It wasn't an invite to come over and work, or to some boring social event that would require a large measure of patience until you could politely leave after a respectable amount of time. The host wasn't asking them to help put an addition on his house, or to help at sheep shearing time, or to help clear rocks out of his field, or to take care of his children for a week. The invitation was to a banquet, to an event of good food, good entertainment, and good conversation with others. Figuratively, this is still the nature of God's invitation today, i.e., to an extremely enjoyable, desirable, and celebratory happening of immense importance.

Not only does God extend this wonderful invitation, but He is also determined that the banquet be well attended. When the first round of invitees bailout in Matthew 22 and Luke 14, servants go out into the streets and alleys and offer an open invitation to anyone who would like to come so that the banquet hall will be full. No one is excluded. Even those who are often forgotten, who are usually not regarded as prime candidates for such a gala event – the poor, the crippled, the blind, and the lame – are invited and encouraged to attend. The only reason for missing the party now will be one's own choice, for God's invitation is open to one and all.

Those who attend are on course for an incredible experience. And what will take place that will ensure that this happens? – principally, the gift that the host will distribute to all who set aside everything else and make the time to be present. Gift bags are part of the landscape at the major music/television/movie awards ceremonies that take place throughout the year. At the Academy Awards, the most desirable bags are given to all nominees in the Best Actor/Actress, Best Supporting Actor/Actress and Director categories. The host is also included. Items that might find their way into these bags include expensive cosmetics, diamond jewelry, designer clothing, the latest high-tech electronic devices, dinners at noted restaurants, lodging at upscale resorts and spas, and luxury cruises and vacations. Trips to Hawaii, Japan, the Caribbean, and even Antarctica have been part of the package in recent years. In some years – are you ready for this – the value of these gift bags has exceeded $200,000! Such an array of "neat stuff" should help to soften the blow of losing in your particular category.

The "gift bag" at God's Banquet is not limited to just a handful of folks, and its value far exceeds any given at the Academy Awards. Everyone who attends receives God's gift bag and, since all are invited (not just A-list celebrities), no one is left out unless they just never bother to show up; or, unless they show up inappropriately attired without the proper humility, dependence upon Christ, and willingness to observe the etiquette and behavior suitable to the occasion which was apparently true of the man in Matthew 22:11-14. And, while no financial value is involved, the gift is of unsurpassed worth.

What is in God's gift bag? The principal item is what we all need – *mercy*. His mercy, offered through the sacrifice of Christ for our sins, makes it possible for us to have fellowship with the Lord and be regarded as friends. Mercy means that God shows compassion and kindness to us in this way: "He does not treat us as our sins deserve or repay us according to our iniquities. . . as far as the east is from the west, so far has he removed our transgressions from us" (Psalm 103:10-12). The biblical message is that a holy and righteous God cannot stand in the presence of sin. Since sin, on some level, is present in each one of us, the result should be that God is forced to avoid us and leave us to our own devices. However, God wasn't satisfied with this scenario and moved to turn everything around, taking care of and removing our sins by sending the sinless Christ who "bore our sins in his body on the tree" (1 Peter 2:24). Instead of receiving what we should have received (separation from God), in Christ we receive mercy.

I have always been amazed at how the Scriptures talk about God's mercy and love. Notice how it is described in the following verses:

> But You, O Lord, are a God full of compassion, and gracious, longsuffering and abundant in mercy and truth (Psalm 86:15, NKJV).

> But from everlasting to everlasting the LORD's love is with those who fear him, and his righteousness with their children's children (Psalm 103:17).

> But because of his great love for us, God who is rich in mercy, made us alive with Christ even when we were dead in transgressions – it is by grace you have been saved. And God raised us up with Christ and seated us with him in the heavenly realms in Christ Jesus, in order that in the coming ages he might show the incomparable riches of his grace, expressed in his kindness to us in Christ Jesus (Ephesians 2:4-7).

> Praise be to the God and Father of our Lord Jesus Christ! In his great mercy he has given us new birth into a living hope through the resurrection of Jesus Christ from the dead (1 Peter 1:3).

Thus, God is rich in mercy, and His mercy is abundant, great, and from everlasting to everlasting. The King James Version uses the word "plenteous" at a couple of points. If you've ever thought that you might be beyond the reaches of God's mercy, jump back and think again. God isn't stingy with His mercy. He doesn't have a limited supply that He has to parcel out only to those we might regard as the most deserving. Truly, there are more than enough gift bags to go around for those who call upon Him.

These realities form a firm foundation for our claim that God is the source of exceeding joy. God's track record of faithfulness is unblemished; in Him, we are never in over our heads in the situations of life; the most powerful being in the universe knows us and thinks about us, cares about us, and desires for good things to happen in our lives; and the wonder of His invitation and mercy is so marvelous and overwhelming. When we live and bask in these realities, we can heartily practice what David encouraged – "let the hearts of those who seek the LORD rejoice" (1 Chronicles 16:10).

THE JOY OF CHRIST
AND SALVATION

"Do not be afraid. I bring you good news of great joy
that will be for all the people. Today in the town of David,
a Savior has been born to you; he is Christ the Lord."

Luke 2:10-11

There are two things we need to keep in mind about the good news that was announced to the shepherds on that star-lit night so long ago. First of all, God set it all in motion. Without his love and initiative, there would be no salvation to talk about, no tidings and good news of great joy. Second, the salvation that God offers comes through the Son, Jesus Christ. "For God so loved the world that he gave his one and only Son, that whoever believes in him shall not perish but have eternal life" (John 3:16). Jesus the Christ, sent by God, comes to our rescue. He, the sinless one, takes our sins upon Himself so that we can appear righteous, without sin or spot, before God.

Many today don't like to own up to any involvement with sin (it's not very contemporary to talk about sin nor very flattering to concede that one has experience in this realm). And, if folks do admit that they haven't always been and done what they should, they don't seem to get overly concerned about it, trusting in an overall goodness to make things right. However, *to be right in the sight of God requires that sin be removed.* Whether it has been a little white lie, not honoring our parents properly when we were teenagers, being less than honest on our income taxes, crude language, gossip, embezzlement, adultery, or murder, *the item has to be erased, not merely counterbalanced with more good things than bad.*

I think our thought process sometimes goes like this: "OK, I haven't always been the person, spouse, son or daughter, parent, friend, church member, neighbor, or employee that I should be, but my pluses outweigh my minuses so I'm all right." For the sake of the argument, even if we have a ratio of 3-1, 10-1, 50-1, or 1,000-1 of positive things over negative ones, the negatives (the sins) are still there. A good ratio may look nice on paper – it provides a way to view ourselves in a favorable light. We're ready for "high fives" and "pats on the back" all around, but the truth is that sin has to be taken away for us to have fellowship with God. And that is exactly what Christ does. He provides what is needed, what we cannot provide or do ourselves. He rescues us, saves us by removing and dealing with our sins, forever – "For Christ died for sins once for all, the righteous for the unrighteous, to bring you to God" (1Peter 3:18a). In essence, Christ saves us, delivers us from the ABC's of sin, i.e., the *allure* of sin, the *bondage* of sin, and the *condemnation* of sin. Let's look at each of these very important categories.

If we are honest, we know that the *allure* of sin can be tremendously powerful. Initially, it promises much in the way of pleasure and excitement ("Aren't you tired of always conforming, denying yourself, and never doing anything 'out of the box'?"). It presents itself as innocent ("Come on, it's no big deal and no one will get hurt"). It convinces us that no one close to us will ever know ("You're too clever for anyone to find out"). It assures us that hordes of other people are doing it (and that those who are not doing it wish that they could). And, it reasons that we can bailout whenever we want ("Don't worry, try it just this once and if you don't like it, just go back to the way things were before"). All of these arguments are seriously flawed because people do get hurt, people do find out, and it's not easy to go back after our peace of mind has been lost, after our reputation has been tainted or ruined, and after our relationships have been strained, perhaps to the breaking point. So, what can be done to beat back these babbling voices that do not have our best interests in mind?

The answer is simple but not necessarily easy to carry out. James reminds us that if we draw near to God, He will draw near to us (for strength, guidance, and help – 4:8a). Also, by coming to Christ, a whole new realm of "newness" opens up. "Therefore, if anyone is in Christ, he is a new creation; the old has gone, the new has come!" (2 Corinthians 5:17). When we truly yield to Christ, His cleansing of sins and salvation take effect, and a new life unfolds. This new life centers on the following:

A New Acknowledgement - Not to pick on men but, like me, you may have read that there are two things that men find hard to do. The first is that we find it hard to admit that we're wrong and say that we're sorry (I guess pride and the macho thing figure in here), and the second is that we find it hard to ask for help (you're going to bring up that "asking for directions" thing, aren't you?). However, in order to deal with the allure of sin and to experience newness in Christ, we have to be able to overcome our reluctance in these areas, whether we are male or female. Giving up our ways and turning to Christ involves coming to the point where we admit our waywardness and express our sorrow for falling down on the job of doing the will of the Lord. This, in turn, is followed up by asking for help, admitting that we cannot manage the living of life on our own.

When we try to do things on our own, too often we end up where we shouldn't be and don't need to be. Near the end of my Navy days, we had a fairly seasoned sailor wander into an establishment that was not going to assist with his character development in any way. He left with two young women who promised a good time. He soon found out that the "good time" involved the use of drugs. Knowing the Navy's "use and lose" drug policy, he still proceeded to party on since he didn't want to disappoint his new companions and come off as a wimp in their eyes. Later, at his command, he was tested for drugs and turned up "positive." The result – all his years of training and experience, his good pay level, and his time accumulated toward retirement were swept away. No longer viewed as a sailor to be trusted to work on a nuclear vessel, he was discharged and sent home. His life changed dramatically because of his moments of indiscretion when he trusted in his own wisdom and gave in to the desire for an off-limits good time.

We need help to live life in the best possible way because moments of decision regarding possible indiscretions continually arise. I have always appreciated a phrase in the account about the beheading of John the Baptist (see Mark 6:17-29). Herodias wanted John out of the picture because of his moral meddling (John plainly stated that Herod should not have his brother Philip's wife). Herod put John in prison but protected him, "knowing him to be a righteous and holy man." Finally, however, "<u>the opportune time came</u>" – an opportunity to end up in a strange and compromising situation. Herod had a birthday and a big birthday bash. No doubt, the alcohol flowed. The daughter of Herodias danced a pleasing dance (we're probably not talking about square dancing or ballroom dancing here). Herod made a rash, ill-advised promise, proclaiming that she could have anything that she wanted, up to half of his kingdom (what in the world was Herod thinking?). After consulting with her mother, the young woman made the highly unexpected request of John's head on a platter (who could have seen that coming – what happened to a nice ring or necklace?). "The king was greatly distressed, but because of his oaths and his dinner guests, he did not want to refuse her" (vs.

26). Herod was caught and, with all eyes staring at him, he did not have the moral courage to back away from such a reprehensible act. He ordered John to be beheaded.

Indeed, the allure of sin is great and opportunities come that put us in the vise between right and wrong, between what will enrich us and what will impoverish us. Without help beyond our own strength and judgment, our chances of ending up in a place that is good for us and pleasing to God are shaky at best. We definitely need a new acknowledgement.

A New Alignment – This, too, is immensely important in dealing with the allure of sin. In Colossians 3:1-3, the apostle Paul wrote: "Since, then, you have been raised with Christ, set your hearts on things above, where Christ is seated at the right hand of God. Set your minds on things above, not on earthly things. For you died, and your life is now hidden with Christ in God." A new focus on the things of God and Christ puts us in a position so that grace and goodness from above can be the main streams that flow through our lives, rather than earthly streams that can lead to slippery footing and undesirable consequences.

Someone will be quick to say that this surely means that any real "fun" will be eliminated from our experience. I beg to differ. Yes, "fun" may take on a different face, but our enjoyment of life actually becomes better since we are no longer trafficking in the titillating, the risqué, the questionable, and the "out-of-bounds" that may rise up to create problems at any time. Newly aligned with "things that are above," what we discover is:

> — we don't have to have a constant barrage of sexual innuendo to have a good laugh (contrary to what a lot of present-day television seems to believe).

> — we don't have to seek out dubious pursuits every Friday and Saturday night to release stress and have a good time.

— we don't have to be a party to "lusting, fussing, and cussing" to show how uninhibited, progressive, and independent we are.

— we don't have to follow the "crowd" and test drive every new "morally challenged" idea or activity to find satisfaction and fulfillment.

The old adage is "that we feel right after we do right." This new alignment will enable us to feel right and good about our ourselves as we focus on and practice the things that will uplift us as we grow more and more in line with the mind of Christ. As a result, we will be much better prepared to deal with the allure of sin and its tantalizing power.

A New Attachment – In Philippians 4:8, we find another vital encouragement from the apostle Paul: "Finally, brothers, whatever is true, whatever is noble, whatever is right, whatever is pure, whatever is lovely, whatever is admirable – if anything is excellent or praiseworthy – think about such things." These words go hand in hand with Paul's thoughts in Romans 12:2a, "Do not conform any longer to the pattern of this world, but be transformed by the renewing of your mind." What we allow our minds to dwell on is a major factor in dealing successfully or unsuccessfully with the allure of sin.

Several years ago when *Dynasty* was riding high in the TV ratings, there was a Frank and Ernest cartoon where the boys where mulling over what to watch. Their conversation went something like this: "We can turn to channel 4 and watch Charleton Heston give the Ten Commandments, or we can turn to channel 6 and watch Joan Collins break the Ten Commandments." That pretty much spells out our options. We can fill our minds with the beneficial and edifying, or we can fill them with the practices and philosophies of this present world that, more than likely, will not benefit and edify us. Only the true, noble, right, pure, lovely, admirable, excellent, and praiseworthy will lead to personnel enrichment and right relationships between us and God, between us and others. Other items may lead to temporary gratification, momentary "highs," or individual advantage but only an attachment to the above virtues will lead us in the "paths of righteousness" whereby we overcome and avoid the complications of misguided thoughts and deeds.

Such an attachment is not always easy to maintain as we go about our daily lives. Some of the talk shows that are presented for our viewing pleasure each day parade a vast amount of dysfunction before us. Likewise, all kinds of sexual, moral, and ethical situations are dealt with on TV and in the movies and presented as commonplace and acceptable, but so many of these situations do not measure up under the scrutiny of Scripture. When we move away from Scripture, what becomes the basis for values and direction? The basis for morality and what people believe appropriate behavior to be becomes individual opinions and human reasoning, rooted in personal desires and agendas, not in any time-honored and proven tradition of what is truly best for us all.

When we fill our minds with the swirl of thinking around us, other than the true, noble, right, pure, etc., our attachments become skewed and drive us into the arms of sexual, moral, and inter-personal confusion.

A New Approach – Another part of the newness that helps us to deal with the allure of sin is also portrayed in Colossians 3. After instructing us to "put to death" such matters as sexual immorality, impurity, lust, evil desire, and greed, and to rid ourselves of anger, rage, malice, slander and filthy language, Paul states the following:

> Therefore, as God's chosen people, holy and dearly beloved, clothe yourselves with compassion, kindness, humility, gentleness and patience. Bear with each other and forgive whatever grievances you may have against

one another. Forgive as the Lord forgave you. And over all these virtues put on love, which binds them all together in perfect unity. Let the peace of Christ rule in your hearts, since as members of one body you were called to peace. And be thankful (vss. 12-15).

While there may be that favorite shirt or pair of jeans that we hate to give up, no matter how old and tattered they have become, in general we all like new clothes. In these verses, Paul describes the new wardrobe of the believer. When a Christian goes to his/her closet in the morning to get ready for the day, items such as "self above all else" and lack of concern for the needs and feelings of others are singularly absent from the ensemble choices. And, the Christian should be coordinated with pieces that fit and match, avoiding any fashion citations for poor judgment when it comes to a sense of style. You wouldn't mix polka dots and plaids, but we mix "I'm here for you" with impatience, or "I'm your friend" with harboring hurts and having grudges. You wouldn't mix floral patterns with stripes, but as Christians we sometimes mix "praise to God" on Sundays with obscenities and backstabbing on Monday, or "my hope is built on nothing less than Jesus' blood and righteousness" with the ruthless pursuit of worldly goods and acclaim. Proper clothing (in the spiritual sense) is very important in the Christian life.

The mainstays of the Christian's wardrobe are compassion, kindness, humility, gentleness, patience, forgiveness, love, peace, and gratitude. Any accessories must blend and mesh with the overall flow of the outfit. Every year at red carpet events, there seem to be a couple of wardrobe choices that prompt us to exclaim, "What in the world was he or she thinking!" As has been said, clothes make the person and so it is with the person seeking to follow Christ. A concern for our spiritual attire is definitely in order.

Hopefully, the above discussion will help to arm us as we battle the *allure* of sin. Our acceptance of Christ and involvement in this "newness" of the Christian life will also help us with the *bondage* of sin and, in turn, the *condemnation* of sin.

What we're getting at when we talk about the *bondage* of sin is simply that it is very easy to become continually subject to its forceful nature and its influence. One of the major problems with sin is that, once we start down that path, we tend to return again and again. Good intentions and resolutions to stay away after "just one more time" are typically ineffective. What results is that all too frequently we end up doing the things that we despise and not doing the good that we desire. The apostle Paul described it in this way:

> So I find this law at work: When I want to do good, evil is right there with me. For in my inner being I delight in God's law; but I see another law at work in the members of my body, waging war against the law of my mind and making me a prisoner of the law of sin at work within my members. What a wretched man I am! Who will rescue me from this body of death? Thanks be to God – through Jesus Christ our Lord! So then, I myself in my mind am a slave to God's law, but in the sinful nature a slave to the law of sin (Romans 7:21-25).

As already mentioned, we need the assistance of the One who adds divine strength and help to our limited human capabilities. Christ is the only answer to this dilemma!

Matthew 12:43-45 and Luke 11:24-26 give us some additional food for thought at this point. In these verses, Jesus talked about removing an evil spirit from a person's life; however, there is no real gain or advantage for the person unless new residents (i.e., the things of God) are installed in the "house" of his or her life. Otherwise, the evil spirit returns with several of his buddies who proceed to take over the unoccupied space, and the situation is even worse than it was before! Bondage to sin can only be overcome by filling our lives with the newness that Christ brings.

This leaves the matter of the *condemnation* of sin. Linked now to Christ and living in Him, "Therefore, there is now no condemnation for those who are in Christ Jesus" (Romans 8:1). Imagine this – in Christ there is no longer any guilt before God; no label of being a despicable wrongdoer and, thus, an outsider in His sight; no judgment handed down that forever exiles us from God's presence. Instead, we are now able to consider ourselves dead to sin and alive to God in Christ Jesus (see Romans 6:11). Without Christ, sin condemns us before God; with Christ, we are able to shout, "What condemnation? I am saved; I appear righteous to God because of Christ who never dabbled in sin, who overcame both sin and death, and who allows His righteousness to be applied to me. He has rescued me and set me on a victorious, heavenly course!"

One of my favorite "rescue" stories centers around the New England whaling industry in the nineteenth century. Back then, there were many families whose life was the sea. Not all of them had good fortune – the sea *gave* a livelihood but, on many occasions, it also *took away*. There was one family whose father went to sea and never returned, his ship caught in a tremendous storm. Later, one of the sons took up the whaling life. One season, his ship put out to sea and was not heard from again. It was presumed that he, too, was lost at sea.

One evening, another furious storm hit the coast. As the terrible, fierce storm raged on, debris from a ship that had broken up began to appear on the shore. Through the dark, black clouds and sky, someone was able to detect a floundering sailor, alive but in great distress. The youngest son of this family dashed to the shore to volunteer to help with the rescue. His mother pleaded with him, "John, don't go. Please don't go. Your father drowned at sea many years ago. Your brother, Luke, went to sea and was never heard from again. Please don't go. I couldn't stand it if anything were to happen to you." But the young man felt compelled and struck off, risking his life to save the lone sailor in need.

Time passed; long, agonizing moments for the mother. Finally, someone came rushing up from the shore bringing news, for good or for ill. "Is he all right?", the mother desperately wanted to know. "Did John make it back?", she inquired frantically. "Yes," said the messenger, "and he said to tell mother that the man is Luke. He said to tell you that the man is your other son."

The young man risked everything to save a fellow human being; as it turned out, to save his brother. He was willing to give his all in a great act of compassion and concern. So it is with Jesus, our Lord. Not only was He willing to risk and to give His all, He actually did so, dying on the cross, bearing our sins so that they would not stand against us and keep us from the Father, the greatest act of compassion and concern the world has ever seen. He did for us what we could not do, what we could never do. He made it possible for God to view us as pure. He made it possible for us to be cleansed and forgiven, breaking down all barriers between us and the Father. He opened up the way for our salvation.

Indeed, Christ is the source of our salvation because He is the only One who can help us deal effectively with the ABCs of sin, with its *allure*, its *bondage*, and its *condemnation*. As we put our trust in Him, our *destiny* also changes from "death" to "eternal life." Without question, this is "good news of great joy" for all people. The "joy of Christ and salvation" should brighten our paths and encourage our hearts every moment of every day.

THE JOY OF FORGIVENESS

"Son, be of good cheer, your sins are forgiven."

Matthew 9:2b (NKJV)

Clarence E. Macartney was a prominent Presbyterian minister of the last century. In his book, *The Greatest Words in the Bible and in Human Speech*, he lists what, for him, are the greatest words and assigns them a descriptive phrase. For instance, Macartney designates "tomorrow" as "the most dangerous word." "Prayer" is viewed as "the word that conquers God," and "come" is regarded as "God's favorite word." Numerous other words are treated in the book, including "the most beautiful word" which Macartney believes to be "forgiveness."

The "joy of forgiveness" flows naturally from our last chapter since salvation and forgiveness are very much intertwined. God's forgiveness means that our sins are no longer part of the equation when determining our relationship with Him; they are no longer part of the spiritual landscape. For those who accept the Lord and seek to live in the Spirit, Christ takes our sins upon Himself and forgives us, leaving us with a clean slate, whole and pure before God. Thus, we are saved not only <u>from</u> sin and death, but we are also saved to friendship and fellowship with God through Christ, both in this life and in the life to come.

While a few other words might contend for the title of "most beautiful," Macartney defends his choice in the following:

> Sin is the saddest word in the Bible and in human speech; but forgiveness is the most beautiful word because it cancels the effects of sin. It takes away the sorrow and the darkness of sin, as the light of the sun scatters the darkness of the night... Forgiveness is the most beautiful word because it kindles the most beautiful light in the face of God or in the countenance of man. It is the most beautiful word because it is the costliest word. Before God could pronounce it Christ had to die on the Cross. It is the word that the Apostles and the angels like to pronounce. It is the word dearest to every true believer. It is the word that will awaken the music of the redeemed in heaven, for that is what they sing about there, the forgiveness of God – "Now unto Him that loved us and hath washed us from our sins by His own blood."[3]

In reality, there are several aspects to biblical forgiveness. We will look at three aspects in this chapter, but the one that probably comes to mind first is this matter of *God's Forgiveness through the Sacrificial Death of Jesus Christ.*

Forgiveness through Christ means that the debt owed for violating God's law has been paid and cancelled through what our Lord did on the cross in dying for us all. We have been pardoned and our guilt has been removed and erased. As humans, we have a tendency to remember, to mentally hang on to our sins since it pains us to know that we have allowed what God abhors to

---

3. Clarence E. Macartney, *The Greatest Words in the Bible and in Human Speech* (Nashville: Cokesbury Press, 1938), 22-23.

enter our lives (note David's experience in Psalm 51:3-4). However, because of Christ, God does not remember or hold onto our offenses against what is good and right; instead, He casts "all our iniquities into the depths of the sea" (Micah 7:19) and remembers them no more (see Isaiah 43:25, Jeremiah 31:34, Hebrews 8:12 and 10:17). While we may continue to beat ourselves up mentally over sins of the past, God is wondering what all the fuss is about since He has no recall of our stumbling, fumbling, bumbling past if we have approached Him with repentant, contrite hearts trusting in the mercy that comes through Christ.

This is the only way to experience true peace in our lives. Counselors may tell us that things of the past are over and done with, just forget them and move on. Doctors may tell us to forgive ourselves and not dwell on these matters anymore. Such advice may be helpful to an extent but, in the end, God is the only One who can ultimately forgive since our misdeeds are against His goodness and righteousness. And, He is the only One who can make our sins go away, through the sacrifice of Christ our Lord. *The search for peace regarding sin and the past will not reach a satisfactory conclusion until God and Christ are recognized as indispensable to the process.*

Peace can elude us for a long time until we appropriate God's grace and allow it to flood into our hearts and minds, letting go of those nagging thoughts that keep saying, "Surely you don't think that God can forgive you?" Several years ago, I was serving as the Deputy Division Chaplain for the 2d Marine Division out of Camp Lejeune, NC.[4] The Division sponsors the 2nd Marine Division Association which is comprised of Marines who have served with the Division in years past. Every year, on the Division's birthday, these Marines return to Camp Lejeune for a couple of days of "homecoming." On a Friday morning, we conducted a Memorial Service

---

4. As a Navy chaplain, I also served with the Marine Corps since Navy chaplains serve all of the "sea services," i.e., the Navy, Marine Corps, and Coast Guard. Navy chaplains also serve at the Merchant Marine Academy.

for those who had given their lives in the great battles and campaigns in the Division's history. We then went to what is called a Battle Colors and Awards Ceremony.

After this second ceremony, a gentleman approached me who needed to talk. I had prayed at these services, and he reached out to me in his need. I could tell that he was visibly shaken, that he was troubled in his mind and spirit. He said that something had been bothering him for a long time and that he wanted to talk with a chaplain. He was a retired Master Sergeant, in his seventies now, who had served in both World War II and Korea.

His problem went back to 1944. He was serving with the Marines on the island of Saipan in the Pacific. The chaplain came by, inviting the young men to services, and he stopped to talk to this man who was probably just a teenager at the time. The chaplain said something to the effect, "What is your faith?" This man, young and cocky, sure of himself and full of himself, responded and said, "Greed." Greed was what he lived for, the essence of his beliefs.

The gentleman survived his war time experiences, grew in maturity, and eventually came to the Lord. However, for fifty-six years, he remembered what he said to the chaplain that day. It bothered him and haunted him, and he couldn't let it go. He couldn't forgive himself, and he needed to tell someone (specifically another chaplain) that this episode had happened when he was young and immature, and he didn't really mean it. He said it just to be smart. Did I think that the chaplain of fifty-six years ago understood and had forgiven him? Did I think that God understood and could forgive him? Did I think that God's grace could cover such an episode such as this?

Our conversation lasted only about fifteen minutes, but I trust that this man went away in the peace of God. I sought to convey that God most certainly could understand and did understand, that He is a forgiving God. God is aware of our humanness. The Psalmist relays, "For he knows how we are formed, and remembers that we are dust" (103:14). This is simply a reference to the creation account indicating that we are men and women formed out of the dust of the earth. Thus, God understands that we are not like the angels or other heavenly beings, and that we are continually contending with our human natures.

Also, John points out that the sacrifice of Christ provides forgiveness for the whole gamut of sin and waywardness – "If we confess our sins, he is faithful and just and will forgive us our sins and purify us from all unrighteousness" (1 John 1:9). In short, even after becoming a Christian (John is writing to Christians here), if we confess and "agree" with God about the need for the cleansing power of Christ, we will be forgiven "all unrighteousness." What have you done that falls outside the range of "all unrighteousness"? That is a pretty all-inclusive term. Emotionally, you may feel that stealing, neglect of family, a misspent youth, adultery, murder, or a hundred other things tax God's ability to forgive, but, from where I sit, they are all included under this umbrella of what God is willing and able to forgive. What you can know is that God's forgiving ability through Christ does not depend on the nature, the number of times, or the length in months and years of what we have done. To God, "all unrighteousness" simply means "all unrighteousness" with no fine print listing a bunch of exceptions!

Sound incredible? Indeed, it does. What we have to remember is that we are dealing with God's forgiveness and not human forgiveness. We tend to look at things from a human perspective which is only natural since that's the basic perspective that we have. However, through Christ, God opens up the way of forgiveness without belittling, without holding grudges, without requiring all kinds of payback or putting us on probation, and without holding it over our heads in the future. His overriding concern is that none perish but that all come to repentance (2 Peter 3:9). It is a love that is extremely difficult to comprehend since it doesn't tend to happen this way in human interaction.

As the Scriptures say, it is a "gift" (Romans 6:23) to be followed by living a life that reflects our love and gratitude. Indeed, "thanks be to God for his indescribable gift" (2 Corinthians 9:15).

These realities are what I shared with the retired Master Sergeant. It seemed to me that a cloud was lifted, that he was finally able to hear and accept God's marvelous offer of forgiveness and peace through Jesus Christ. After we prayed, I believe he went on his way with a great burden lifted.

His experience is not uncommon. I have encountered many, many individuals over the years who have heard the message of forgiveness but find it hard to emotionally accept the fact that it actually covers their individual situation. They believe that God can forgive others, but it's just too much to believe that God can forgive whatever it is that they have done. The need is to let go of thinking that we are an exception, that our case is somehow different and that we, out of everyone else on the planet, somehow challenge God's capacity to forgive. David was forgiven of several major miscues (e.g., murder and adultery). Peter was incorporated back into the circle of followers after denying our Lord. Paul, the "chief/worst/foremost" of sinners (1 Timothy 1:15) in his mind, was forgiven the times he persecuted the church. Through Christ, God wants us to be free of guilt and internal turmoil, and He has made it possible to know peace and joy. It truly is as Peter conveyed to the household of Cornelius, ". . . everyone who believes in him [Christ] receives forgiveness of sins through his name" (Acts 10:43). We need to trust Peter and the Word. Peter would know on the human level about the all-encompassing power of forgiveness through Christ, and God never says anything that He doesn't mean.

The remaining two areas surrounding forgiveness center on forgiveness as it plays out in our interpersonal relationships. According to our Lord, *Forgiving Others who Have Sinned Against Us or in Some Way Offended Us is a Crucial Quality of the Christian Life*. Most of us are familiar with the Lord's Prayer in Matthew 6 and Luke 11. If we have paid attention to the prayer and not just routinely recited its contents, we realize that our own forgiveness is linked to our forgiveness of others. Here is what Jesus said in Matthew 6:12, 14-15: "Forgive us our debts, as we also have forgiven our debtors. . . For if you forgive men when they sin against you, your heavenly Father will also forgive you. But if you do not forgive men their sins, your Father will not forgive your sins." From our earlier discussion about the Christian's wardrobe, we recall that Paul reinforced this emphasis in Colossians 3:13b when he talked about bearing with one another and forgiving each other – "Forgive as the Lord forgave you."

Why is a willingness to forgive so important in the Christian life? Obviously, since Christians are those who are trying to be like Christ, a forgiving spirit is essential to any kind of modeling of Christ's values and outlook ("Your attitude should be the same as that of Christ Jesus," Philippians 2:5). One of the major complaints (or in a lot of cases, "excuses") that outside people have regarding the Church is that there is often an inconsistency between what our Lord encourages and what Christians actually practice. Our love, compassion, morality, language, etc., may sometimes be lacking when measured against what the world expects of Christians. Certainly, as human beings, we are not perfect and there will be times when we lapse and error, that's why we say that the primary focus should be on Christ, not on us, since there is no disappointment in Him. However, the world should still be able to see Christ reflected in us as we earnestly seek to follow in His ways.

My last tour as a chaplain was with submarines. Since the number of sailors on a fast attack submarine does not support a permanently assigned chaplain (myself and another chaplain covered three squadrons of six submarines each), we trained lay leaders to conduct lay services and hold up matters of faith when the boats went to sea. In our training, we talked about integrity and setting a good moral example. I jokingly used to say that, as representatives of the Lord, we expect that lay leaders won't be running a drug ring about the ship and that the proverbial "swearing like a sailor" label will in no way apply. While said in jest, the point is that there should not be a great chasm between what we are saying and representing, and what we are doing. While there may be slipups, our lives need to reflect a concentrated effort to model our Lord and Savior. A forgiving spirit is definitely among the qualities that should be evident in our treatment of others.

There are numerous other reasons as to why a forgiving spirit for others is encouraged upon us. When we harbor and brood over alleged offenses, it directs our energy into negative channels. Our thoughts then focus on such matters as resentment, anger, or revenge which will not enable us to end up in any healthy place regarding the emotional, mental, spiritual, and even physical aspects of our lives. Our lives will be out of sync since we are emphasizing and even seeking the negative about others. Once we start down this path, the tendency is to continue to look for more ammunition, more of the negative, so that we can continue to justify the position that we have taken. This is no way to live, unless we are purposely seeking to rob ourselves of the joy of the Lord and to be of no use to others or to ourselves.

As followers of Christ, we also need to allow some "wiggle room" for the actions of others. Maybe the person who has supposedly offended us did not intend the matter as we took it (yes, we might have been off in our interpretation). Maybe they were having an off day and were not fully up to par. Maybe they were dealing with some other issues (e.g., stress at work or home) that spilled over into what they said or did. Maybe they have not had the same advantages and experiences that we have had and, therefore, have a different idea as to what is appropriate and acceptable (we can't expect others to always think and respond as we do).

Beyond this, even if something has been done willfully and spitefully against us, we do not want to be drawn into living and responding in a similar manner. To respond on the same level means that the cycle of bitterness and alienation will continue, that we will reap strife and contention perhaps for a long time to come, and that our faith has stalled in responding. Letting go of the matter and making the first move to patch things up does not mean that we have become weak and spineless. It merely means that, in Christ, we see the senselessness of holding on to questionable personal offenses and that there is no worthwhile value in allowing them to fester. It merely means that we are striving to walk in a way that is better for all concerned and that allows the light of Christ to shine through.

That last Navy assignment was in Connecticut where a lot of rocks and boulders dot the landscape. During a presidential election while we were there, I drove past a home where the owner had painted an encouragement on a huge rock at the end of his/her driveway for a particular candidate. As it turned out, "the candidate of the rock" lost. I wondered what this homeowner would do with this message that was still there in bold letters after the election for all the world to see. Would he/she just leave it there as a protest against those who voted otherwise? Would he/she paint over it with a new message, something spiteful like, "You'll see I was right" or "What were you thinking?" I drove past this home a couple of weeks later. The message had changed. Now it read, "God bless the USA." For our Christian witness and our own health and well-being, we need to pick up and move on from situations that disappoint us, challenge us personally, and don't turn out to our liking. The Christian does so in the strength of the Holy Spirit.

Before leaving these thoughts about forgiving others, we might ask, "Just what does it mean to forgive someone else?" Does it mean that we forget what has taken place as in "forgive and forget"? Does it mean that we let them back into our good graces after they spend some time begging and groveling? Does it mean that we treat them kindly again but always have something to hold over their head and use against them in the future?

Actually, none of these approaches provide us with the right answer.

It would be good if we could forget some of the things that happen, but thoughts and experiences linger in our minds. Thus, we strive to avoid dwelling on the episodes that recall irritation and friction; we strive to redirect our thoughts to beneficial avenues when such episodes rise to the surface. Likewise, begging and groveling will not permit both parties to experience acceptance and self-dignity in a relationship. The groveling one will always feel subordinate and inferior. And, if a relationship has presumably been restored, none of us like for items of the past to be brought up later and used as a hammer against us. I've always remembered a cartoon that appeared in the Reader's Digest several years ago. A husband and wife were in their bedroom, apparently having an argument. The wife was sitting up in bed while the husband was standing over by the wall where there was a long line of filing cabinets. In the caption, the wife says, "For once, I wish we could have a discussion without you going to the files." This disruptive tendency has come up over and over again in my counseling through the years.

If none of these options depict forgiveness, what does? The late Dallas Willard once wrote that "we forgive someone of a wrong they have done us when we decide that we will not make them suffer for it in any way."[5] In short, the silent treatment, sleeping on the couch for a week, requiring something so that the other person makes it up to us, cutting loose with angry and hurtful words, etc., are not part of the picture. As we have talked about, this isn't God's approach to forgiveness, and it shouldn't be our approach either. Relationships and friendships are too precious, too important, too valuable to risk merely so that we can save face or get what we think is owed to us. True forgiveness and devising ways to make the offender miserable do not mix.

---

5. Dallas Willard, *The Divine Conspiracy: Rediscovering our Hidden Life in God* (San Francisco: HarperSan-Francisco, 1998), 262.

The final aspect of forgiveness centers on *Our Need, at Times, to Seek the Forgiveness of Others in Order to Make Things Right and Bring about Healing.* Believe it or not, there are times when we are the one who has lapsed and turned in a not so stellar performance that is disappointing or hurtful to another. Given our humanity, it is bound to happen.

When Christine was about six or seven, we decided it was time to get some new sheets for her bed. Off we went to the mall to track something down. As we surveyed the possibilities, a problem developed – not for Christine but for me (this is not one of my shining moments; to this day, I have never figured out what got into me). The problem was that Christine liked the sheets with stripes while I liked the sheets with flowers. I thought they were prettier and, after all, shouldn't a young girl have flowered sheets? All of my adult reasoning and persuasiveness couldn't turn the tide. Finally, Christine began to cry. Even a discussion in a side aisle, out of the view of curious passersby, didn't change her choice. We ended up going home without either the stripes or the flowers.

After we got home, the Holy Spirit began a full-scale assault on my conscience. "What in the world did you just do? What difference does it make whether Christine selects stripes or flowers for her sheets? They are intended to be her sheets, not yours. This is hardly an ethical matter; right and wrong isn't part of this picture at all. Why can't you let her choose what she wants?" And, so, I apologized, told Christine that I was sorry, and the next day we went back to the store and got the sheets that she wanted. The end of this very unflattering story is that, many years later, we still have the top sheet of that set. It is worn thin and has long since served its usefulness. However, every time Judy wants to throw it away, I hold on to it as a nostalgic reminder of those years when our children were at home, but more so as a reminder that sometimes my brain turns to jelly and I need to seek the forgiveness of others. Others aren't always the culprit. As adults, it can be hard to accept this reality.

In closing this chapter, I am reminded of what Dr. Phil of television talk show fame often says. When people continue in patterns of behavior that result in discord and tension, he is prone to say, "How is that working for you?" In order to get different results, a new approach must be adopted. In the same vein, how does holding on to our guilt, refusing to forgive and harboring grudges, and being too proud to ask for forgiveness when we have messed up work for us? *The honest answer is that it works terrible!* We limp along with a lack of peace, with strained relationships, and with the negative shoving aside the positive in our lives. Joy eludes us.

Let us be thankful that God through Christ offers us a different way with different results. Forgiveness through what Christ has done replaces estrangement between us and God. The healing of relationships, motivated by His example and encouragement, replaces estrangement between us and others. The way of biblical forgiveness is the path that truly leads to joy and peace in our lives!

THE JOY OF THE HOLY SPIRIT

"And hope does not disappoint us, because God has
poured out his love into our hearts by the Holy Spirit,
whom he has given us."

Romans 5:5

Preachers are constantly on the lookout for good stories and illustrations
for their sermons. They can pop up unexpectedly, almost anywhere. While
out shopping one day, I came across a rather unusual little volume in the
bookstore, *The Book of Useless Information*. I couldn't resist browsing
through it and, ultimately, took it home (after paying for it, of course). Did
you know, for instance, that:

— the wheel on the game show Wheel of Fortune is
102 inches in diameter.

— Stewardesses is the longest word that is typed with
only the left hand.

— on average, there are 178 sesame seeds on each
McDonald's Big Mac bun.

— in Texas, it is illegal to put graffiti on someone else's cow.

— Maine is the toothpick capital of the world.

— a baseball has exactly 108 stitches (you might want to remember some of these tidbits for watching Jeopardy on TV).

— the life expectancy of the average mockingbird is ten years.

— it would take 150 years to drive a car to the sun.

— the average person keeps old magazines for twenty-nine weeks before they throw them out (how they know this is beyond me).[6]

We could go on and on – the book covers 286 pages. However, here is a piece of information that is far from useless and that you might not be fully aware of – *the Holy Spirit provides a very vital ministry and a significant presence in our lives.* This reality, in turn, results in great joy in our lives.

Why begin our chapter on the Holy Spirit in this way? Principally, because I think the Holy Spirit sometimes gets lost in the shuffle and is underrated in our Christian experience. Yes, we are aware of the Holy Spirit, but we seem to have a more intimate relationship with God and Christ since God is our heavenly Father and Creator, and Christ is our Savior. And, we simply may not fully understand the role of the Holy Spirit as we live out our Christian lives. I once heard a preacher comment that, since we don't always know how to treat the Spirit, we may tend to think and operate as if He is on vacation somewhere in Brazil. Obviously, this was said with tongue-in-cheek, but it does emphasize that a better understanding might possibly be in order.

6. Noel Botham and the Useless Information Society, *The Book of Useless Information* (New York: The Berkley Publishing Group, 2006), 55, 81, 88, 125, 164, 175, 243, 278, 279.

Our need of the Holy Spirit arises out of the fact that Christ is no longer with us as He was with the first disciples in the first century. Upon Christ's return to glory, we could easily slip into a state of panic since it would be natural to conclude that we are now on our own without His encouragement, strength, and presence. In fact, the early disciples seem to have entertained such thoughts because Jesus had to explain to them that "it is for your good that I am going away" (John 16:7a). However, God had already prepared for a seamless transition through the ministry of the Holy Spirit – "Unless I go away, the Counselor will not come to you; but if I go, I will send him to you" (John 16:7b). No need to fret; as always, God is a step ahead, on top of the situation.

In addition to these words in John 16, Jesus also talked about this just a couple of chapters earlier in John's gospel:

> If you love me, you will obey what I command. And I will ask the Father, and he will give you another Counselor to be with you forever – the Spirit of truth. The world cannot accept him, because it neither sees him nor knows him. But you know him, for he lives with you and will be in you. I will not leave you as orphans; I will come to you (John 14:15-18).

Throw out the "Woe is us, what will become of us now" outlook. Christ will still be with us in the Holy Spirit who will continue to provide all we need for our spiritual lives.

What is it, then, that we need to know about the Holy Spirit that will help us to constantly live in His presence and power? There are numerous aspects of the ministry of the Spirit and, as I survey what God's Word has to say about this important matter, they tend to begin with the letter C. In no particular order, let's see what we can discover about the Holy Spirit that will wonderfully enhance our Christian lives and lead to joy.

Based on Romans 8:26-27, our first *C* is the word *Converts*. While the Holy Spirit has a role in conversion, this is not the emphasis here. In Romans 8, the reference is to the fact that the Holy Spirit *converts our prayers into appropriate requests and communication with God*:

> In the same way, the Spirit helps us in our weakness. We do not know what we ought to pray, but the Spirit himself intercedes for us with groans that words cannot express. And he who searches our hearts knows the mind of the Spirit, because the Spirit intercedes for the saints in accordance with God's will.

With each of our *C*s, the Holy Spirit is going to intercede and intervene for us, to help us in some way. Here, as the Spirit generally helps us as we live in hope awaiting salvation (see vss. 22-25), He also specifically helps us in prayer. Why? Basically, because in our humanness, we have difficulty putting things together and getting things right, which is, likewise, true of prayer. Our "weakness" spills over into prayer in the sense that we do not always know how to go about prayer or how to pray effectively. Certain situations may overwhelm us to the point that we don't even know how we should pray about the matter. Or, in contrast to the Spirit who always prays and intercedes "in accordance with God's will," our will and desires may sometimes eke into the mix and confuse things. The Spirit filters out inappropriateness and filters in appropriateness, so that our prayers receive the hearing that they should before the Father.

Perhaps what happens here is akin to trying to remember and sing a favorite song, hymn, or chorus. We all know what can happen at this point (my family likes to remind me of my shortcomings in remembering lyrics). We're trying to sing an oldie that we like or a hymn or chorus that we've heard in church, but we can't quite come up with all of the words. So, we sing a few words and then throw in a lot of "la-la-las" until we remember the next sequence of words. For instance, maybe we're trying to *Joyful, Joyful, We Adore Thee* as we move through the day. If we can't remember all the words, it may sound something like this:

> Joyful, joyful, we adore Thee,
> God of glory, Lord of love,
> La-la-la-la-la-la-la-la,
> La-la-la-la-la, la-la.
> Melt the clouds of sin and sadness,
> La-la-la-la-la, la-la.
> Giver of immortal gladness,
> Fill us with the light of day.[7]

Our singing, then, is filled with gaps in knowing or remembering, or maybe we even throw in some words that don't belong. Maybe the end result is not verse one but a combination of verses one and three or something that we just made up.

Similarly, our prayers, as far as the Spirit is concerned, may be intertwined with a number of "la-la-las," either because we don't know what to pray in a given situation or because we use some words/thoughts that detract from what we are really trying to say and accomplish, viz., thoughts that lean toward the selfish or spiritually shallow. Processed through the Holy Spirit, we know that our prayers will be formatted appropriately for the best possible hearing with God. What a blessing it is to know that the Spirit is always helping us with our prayers – sorting through what we are trying to say, weeding out any inappropriateness, and letting the Father know of our true spiritual intent. Whether you are new to prayer and aren't sure just how

---

7. The words used from this hymn are taken from Kenneth W. Osbeck, *Amazing Grace: 366 Inspiring Hymn Stories for Daily Devotions* (Grand Rapids, MI: Kregel Publications, 1990), 139.

to go about it, or whether you have been a person of prayer for some time, remember the Spirit is there to help.

Another feature of the Holy Spirit's ministry in us and for us is the word *Confirms*. This thought is based on Ephesians 1:13-14:

> And you also were included in Christ when you heard the word of truth, the gospel of your salvation. Having believed, you were marked in him with a seal, the promised Holy Spirit, who is a deposit guaranteeing our inheritance until the redemption of those who are God's possession – to the praise of his glory.

The presence of the Holy Spirit in our lives *confirms that we are part of the family of God and that we are one of His own.*

Confirmation brings confidence and assurance in the spiritual realm as it does in other areas. If we are traveling, it is reassuring to know that we have a confirmed seat on a flight or a confirmed reservation at a hotel or motel. I remember trying to find a motel room one time when we did not have a reservation. It so happened that there was a big softball tournament in the area and rooms were booked for miles around. Judy and I finally found a place to stay but only after driving many more miles than we had planned.

I remember another time when we did have reservations, but they were not quite on target. I carry a pocket calendar in my wallet from several years ago because it has three inches measured on the side – you never know when you'll need to measure an inch or two. Back when the year had just changed and this calendar was now outdated, I made some reservations that were, unfortunately, based on the old calendar. Obviously, confusion reigned until we were finally able to set things straight. The spiritual lesson here is that we should not depend on inaccurate items to confirm our standing with God and Christ, e.g., our feelings or what others say who may be uninformed. We should only look to the Word and to the Holy Spirit for such confirmation.

According to Paul, the Holy Spirit is God's way of marking us; proof that we are His sons and daughters. As other writers have pointed out, seals were used in the ancient world to guarantee the origin, ownership, protection, and authenticity of the contents of a letter, package, or cargo shipment. In like fashion, the Holy Spirit is the seal that authenticates that we truly belong to God and Christ. Having the presence and power of the Spirit (given as we commit to Christ and begin the Christian life) leaves no doubt that God is with us and doing all that He can to see us through this present life.

Paul presents another interesting concept when he says that the Holy Spirit is also "a deposit guaranteeing our inheritance. . .". In essence, the Holy Spirit is a portion, a down payment for the present for what we will receive in full in glory. Just as a guest speaker might be given a portion of his/ her full honorarium in advance (perhaps to cover travel and initial expenses as a pledge that the complete payment will be made after the event), so the Holy Spirit is God's pledge that our experience of life in the Spirit here is only a foretaste of what is to come when we are ushered into His eternal presence. The Holy Spirit enables us to lead an overcoming life now that will be followed by an overwhelming life then, in heaven. This *confirming* ministry of the Spirit greatly multiples our confidence as God's children and, thus, our joy in the life we live in Him.

Next, the word *Counsels* comes into play – the Holy Spirit *counsels us as we move through the challenges of life.* As mentioned above in John 14:16, Christ promised to send the Spirit as "another Counselor" upon His earthly departure and, of course, He did. The word that John uses in this instance for "Counselor" is not what we typically think of when we hear this designation today; therefore, we need to do a little background study to see exactly what is being said at this point.

When we think of a counselor, the tendency is to call to mind a therapist or someone we go to in order to talk over difficulties while seeking some way for improving or resolving the matters at hand. Maybe you've heard the story about the couple who went on a Caribbean cruise and paid another full passage so that their dog could go, too. When asked why they would pay a full fare for their dog, they replied, "Well, Brownie can't stand to be away from us, and it's cheaper than paying for his therapy when we get back." While counselors can be very helpful, this is not the kind of counseling that John has in mind.

In the original Greek, the word that John uses here is *parakletos*, or "paraclete." It refers to someone who is "called in" or "called alongside." Often, in Greek literature, it is used of a court setting where a person lacks the proper expertise for what is happening and needs someone to guide and help them through the proceedings, watching out for their best interests and protection. Doesn't this fit our situation quite accurately? Many times, we lack the expertise for dealing with what confronts us. Left to our own understanding or to our own limited means who knows how things might turn out – probably not in our favor. Aware of this, Christ sends the Holy Spirit to come alongside with expert counsel and assistance.

In these chapters of preparation for His departure, Jesus mentions some other things that the Paraclete will do in guiding and watching out for us, particularly as we contend for the faith. Truth is a major concern for Christians and for reaching out to others in today's world. Good news! – the Holy Spirit is "the Spirit of truth" (see John 14:16, 15:26, and 16:13). Truth has fallen on hard times in recent decades. Instead of universal truths (ideas that are true across the board for everyone at all times), we now have the nonsense and chaos of individual truth – "this is what is true for me, what I determine to be true; something else may be true for you but, if it is, don't bother me with it." A few years ago, the term "true truth" was tossed around because there were so many opinions and options for truth. Often, what is hyped as truth today does not involve any God-given or time-proven reality and certainty but merely requires that something sound good or feel good so that it can be passed off and taken for truth, often by those who want to alter or ignore the truth for their own purposes. I guess it's sort of like spiritual/philosophical horseshoes; however, I have never held the opinion that closeness counts in the matter of truth.

As we interact with this dilemma, the Holy Spirit is there to guide us into the truth (again, the John 16:13 verse). As we devote ourselves to God, Christ, and the Word, the Holy Spirit is there to light up and implant the truth within us. He, also, "will teach you all things and will remind you of everything I have said to you" (the John 14:26 verse). After Jesus went back to the Father, the early disciples had all kinds of things swirling around in their heads regarding their time with the Lord – events, sayings, sermons, experiences. What did they all mean? How did everything fit together? What needed to be shared with others? The Holy Spirit would help them to sort things out (see John 2:13-22 as an example), just as He continues to help disciples today.

Then, as a counselor, or someone who comes alongside to guide and assist, the Holy Spirit is there for testifying. Since a significant part of the Spirit's work is to testify of Christ, He is present when opportunities arise for us to testify, too (see John 15:27). Thus, we are empowered for situations where it would be precarious to be on our own – empowered for knowing Christ and the truth; empowered for sharing Christ and the truth with the world. There is great joy in having the Holy Spirit as our counselor.

In line with these thoughts, another part of the work of the Holy Spirit is that He *Convicts* – the Holy Spirit *convicts "the world of guilt in regard to sin and righteousness and judgment"* (John 16:8). The world apart from God needs to know that it is off-course when it comes to right and wrong and the ideas it constantly promotes about how to live life; and, from John 16, it needs to know that it is off-course in what it often professes about Christ. Working through the Church and God's people who comprise the Church, the Holy Spirit sets the record straight and exposes the errors that are laced throughout the world's thinking.

After the statement of John 16:8, Jesus continued by saying this convicting ministry of the Spirit will be "in regard to sin, because men do not believe in me; in regard to righteousness, because I am going to the Father, where you can see me no longer; and in regard to judgment, because the prince of this world now stands condemned" (vss. 9-11). The world of Jesus' day (and, unfortunately, often today) thought that it could dismiss Him. It pretty much thought that death would end His notoriety, and He would be just another passing figure on the stage of history. However, the conquering Christ changed all of this. He cannot be dismissed – how do you dismiss someone who, of all the billions who have lived on earth, is the *only one ever* to overcome death? It would be wrong do to so. Instead of being held by death, He arose and ascended back to the Father proving that He is God's Son, the Righteous One, and the Judge of all things (having overpowered and condemned Satan), rather than someone judged to be hardly worthy of a second thought.

Far from a passing, inconsequential figure, He is the central figure in the history of human-kind. He is supremely worthy – no more should we be skeptical or dismissive, only believe. The empty tomb holds up His divinity and righteousness. Satan has been exposed and judged, and Christ will come again as the judge of the living and the dead (see Acts 10:42). All of this is right and true, and the Holy Spirit ministers through us and with us in convicting the world of these realities regarding the Savior.

The world needs to be set straight about our Lord. It also, as indicated above, needs to be set straight about its ways in general. Do you ever watch the game show, *The Price is Right*? Whenever I do, I always get a kick out of the contestants turning to the audience for help when the audience is as clueless as them. For instance, when they're trying to figure out the five numbers in the price of a new car, my contention is that someone might help them with the first two numbers (those numbers might be fairly consistent, within a limited range for a given model), but no one knows the last three numbers, even if they just bought a new car yesterday. It all depends on the equipment of each car and what that equipment costs. Instead of listening to a lot of screaming people shouting out a bunch of guesses, the contestant just needs to pick the final numbers and hope for the best.

Isn't this how it works with the world? Apart from the wisdom of God, the world is clueless, but that doesn't stop it from speaking out with authority and conviction. However, the world is continually confused about right and wrong, about what is appropriate for life and how it should be lived. The world tends to operate on the basis of what feels good, what demands little, what is personally advantageous. Consequently, it is constantly landing on and shouting out misguided opinions, guesses, and advice. Sadly, large numbers of people take it onboard as useful and worthwhile information. To assist with this mixed-up situation, Christ sends the Holy Spirit to aid in convicting and convincing. There is great joy in knowing that we are not on our own for such interaction with the world, but awesome power is available through the Spirit for bringing the world, and us, to the truth.

Two *C*s remain. We would be remiss if we did not remember that the Holy Spirit *Comforts* – the Spirit *comforts us in all our troubles*. This phrase occurs in 2 Corinthians 1:4 and refers to God's comforting presence. However, His means of doing so is through the work of the Holy Spirit who is in us and with us at all times.

How else do we know that the Spirit provides comfort for times when the wind picks up and storms come on the seas of life? Because the Spirit is with us to continue the work of Christ and our Lord was all about bringing comfort to those He encountered who were in need. Peter, who had lived with Jesus over three years and knew His ways like few others, encourages us to "cast all your anxiety on him because he cares for you" (1 Peter 5:7).

Peter had seen Christ caring for people and comforting them, time after time. It happened during times of mourning, as with Mary and Martha (John 11:17-44), Jairus (Luke 8:40-42, 49-52), and the widow whose only son had died, leaving her to face an uncertain and frightening future alone (Luke 7:11-17). It happened with those who were outcasts, either by being unclean (Luke 17:11-19) or sinful and scorned (Luke 7:36-50). It happened with those who were drained of finances from dealing for years with a blood disorder that doctors could not cure (Luke 8:42b-48), and with those who had been ill for decades (John 5:1-15). It happened with those who were possessed (Matthew 15:21-28 and 17:14-21), and it even happened with tough, seasoned men who lived their lives on the sea but were terrified in the midst of a storm (Mark 4:35-41 and 6:45-52).

In many of these cases, Jesus provided comfort through healing; always, He provided comfort through acceptance, encouragement, and hope by His calming, concerned, and interested presence. If needed, He provided forgiveness. I like what Jesus said when the disciples were caught in a storm on the Sea of Galilee and He came to them, walking on the water. To these burly, frightened men, He said, "Take courage! It is I. Don't be afraid" (Mark 6:50). Circumstances may not dissipate as quickly for us as they did on this occasion for the disciples (sometimes, circumstances have to run their course); but, now, in the midst of whatever is swirling around us, there is the comforting and reassuring Christ, injecting acceptance, encouragement, forgiveness, hope, and the strength of His divine presence into what may have seemed hopeless, with despair as the only option just moments before. Let us remember these words, "Take courage – It is I – Don't be afraid," for they truly transform our circumstances. Let us also remember that, according to Luke 7:13, when the Lord saw the widow whose only son had died, "his heart went out to her...". This is still what happens today through the ministry of the Holy Spirit.

And, so, the Holy Spirit *converts, confirms, counsels, convicts, and comforts.* Finally, there is the word – *Coordinates.* When we truly live in the Holy Spirit, I believe that the Spirit *coordinates our paths so that our Christian life is a rich, fulfilling, and victorious experience.*

A development that has arisen in recent years and keeps growing is the dependence on an event planner for special occasions. Take weddings as an example. The wedding planner is there to guide a couple through all the details leading up to the actual occasion. He/she knows when the invitations should be ordered and how far in advance the gown needs to be fitted. The planner knows about such things as florists, photographers, and reception halls. Yielding to the minister for the actual elements of the ceremony, the wedding planner is there the day of the ceremony to guide the ushers, to see that the wedding party gets to their proper places on time, and, at the end, to arrange the receiving line (something hardly anyone is ever sure of). Hopefully, he/she knows how to deal with pushy family members so that the "big day" is what the bride and groom desire, not what someone else desires. The planner knows what is appropriate and inappropriate and knows pitfalls along the way. When all is said and done, he/she ensures that things go well, as they are supposed to go.

As a *coordinator,* the Holy Spirit carries out many of these same functions, spiritually, for us. He knows about guiding our lives for the best possible results. He knows what is appropriate and inappropriate and how best to conduct things. The Spirit knows how things are supposed to go and, in moments of stress (just as there can be with planning a wedding), He is there to help us negotiate the bumps in the road and keep us going. We are not left on our own for the mammoth undertaking of living life but have a life planner, a divine coordinator for guiding and sorting it all out. The end result, when we heed the voice of the Spirit and rely on His powerful, indwelling presence, will be a life well-lived and one that is approved by God.

As we can see, the Holy Spirit is with us to aid us in multiple ways and situations. The Spirit desires to enhance our lives over and over with guidance, assistance, and strength. Indeed, let us rejoice and be glad because great is the ministry of the Holy Spirit for seeing us wonderfully and powerfully through the days of our earthly lives.

THE JOY OF WORSHIP

"Shout for joy to the LORD, all the earth. Serve the LORD
with gladness; come before him with joyful songs."

Psalm 100:2

After considering the themes of the last several chapters, a natural next
step is to look at "the joy of worship." For all that God has done for us
spiritually through Christ and the Holy Spirit (and for all aspects of His
majesty and goodness), we desire to praise His Holy Name and let Him
know that we are profoundly grateful. This is done, in large measure, through
worship.

Our goal in this chapter is not to look at forms and styles of worship
in an attempt to arrive at some conclusion of how worship should best be
conducted in the contemporary church. Forms and styles are very important
and need to be addressed, especially when "worship as entertainment" and
"worship as personal edification" vie for attention among us. Many others
have addressed these issues and have provided us with outstanding "food
for thought." Rather, our goal is to take a basic look at worship and to glean
some guiding principles that will lead to joy in our worship experience.

Corporate worship (which is our main focus here – the Church at worship) can be conducted in a variety of ways and still be meaningful and authentic. However, there are some foundational guidelines that can be kept in mind so that joy and gladness truly result. Our discussion will not be exhaustive, but I trust it will be helpful in pursuing this goal of joy in worship.

Richard C. Leonard states that "worship may serve many purposes in the life of the worshiper,"[8] to include spiritual development, the cultivation of Christian graces, the deepening of understanding, emotional release, the healing of hurts through the touch of the divine, communion with God, thanksgiving to God for benefits received and rejoicing in His presence, individual acts of commitment to serve God, and the corporate celebration of the covenant community. Leonard goes on to add this: "While worship may be all these things, biblical worship operates in an added dimension. For in all these things the focus is on the worshiper; in genuine biblical worship, the focus is always on the One who is worshiped."[9]

This, actually, may be a new, even revolutionary, thought in our thinking about worship. For some, while going back to the parking lot after attending worship, the prevailing thought may be along the lines of "Well, I didn't really get much out of the service today" or "The service didn't really move me a whole lot this morning." Even if the thoughts are positive, an emphasis on how the service affected me may still predominate: "The service today was really great – it really inspired and uplifted me" or "I was really touched by today's singing and preaching." Hopefully, various personal blessings like those mentioned above will result from gathering together to praise and honor God, but the main goal of worship is to glorify the Father and to "worship in spirit and in truth" (John 4:24). The goal is not for us to critique how worship

---

8. Richard C. Leonard, "The Numinous Aspect of Biblical Worship," in *The Biblical Foundations of Christian Worship*, vol. 1, ed. Robert E. Webber (Peabody, MA: Hendrikson Publishers, Inc., 1993), 71.
9. Ibid.

went for us, but for us to concern ourselves with how the worship went for Him, on what did we contribute to His honor and glory.

Against this background, there are a couple of biblical images that surface that help us to maintain this proper perspective in worship. One of these images involves "bowing down/ kneeling" before the divine. Psalm 95:6 states: "Come, let us bow down in worship, let us kneel before the LORD our Maker; for he is our God and we are the people of his pasture, the flock under his care." In Isaiah 45:23b, the Lord declares: "Before me every knee will bow; by me every tongue will swear," which is echoed in that soaring passage in Philippians 2:5-11. Here, while equal with God, Christ Jesus humbled Himself, took on our human form, "and became obedient to death – even death on a cross! Therefore, God exalted him to the highest place and gave him the name that is above every name, that at the name of Jesus every knee should bow in heaven and on earth and under the earth, and every tongue confess that Jesus Christ is Lord, to the glory of God the Father." Clearly, these and other references to "kneeling/bowing down" (e.g., Ephesians 3:14) remind us that the focus in worship belongs to the One who is worthy and who has done so much for us, not on those of us who are kneeling and offering up our adoration, praise, and allegiance.

This matter of being "worthy" is another image that informs a proper concept of worship. Such terms as "worth-ship/worthiness/ascribing worth" are central to the meaning of worship. In both 2 Samuel 22:4 and Psalm 18:3, David says: "I will call to the LORD, who is worthy of praise, and I am saved from my enemies." Singing in heaven proclaims, "You are worthy, Our Lord and God, to receive glory and honor and power, for you created all things, and by your will they existed and were created" (Revelation 4:11). The Lamb is also accorded great acclaim as "ten thousand times ten thousand" angels sing in a loud voice, "Worthy is the Lamb, who was slain, to receive power and wealth and wisdom and strength and honor and glory and praise!" (Rev. 5:11-12).

There are many notable people whose names we know because of prominence in such areas as politics, entertainment, sports, law, medicine, literature, etc. I once had the privilege of meeting and shaking the hand of President George Herbert Walker Bush who visited the military base where I was stationed. It was a great thrill. However, the One who exceeds everyone else and is worthy of worship is the Triune God.

As we would expect, it is interesting to note that bowing down to anyone or anything else is strictly forbidden in Scripture. Early on in the Ten Commandments, God specifically spells this out in Exodus 20:3-5a: "You shall have no other gods before me. You shall not make for yourself an idol in the form of anything in heaven above or on the earth beneath or in the waters below. You shall not bow down to them or worship them; for I, the LORD your God, am a jealous God, . . .". There is little doubt as to why we are so admonished. Isaiah and others point out the true nature of anything else that we would worship, viz., that they are inferior, useless, unable to see or hear or speak, incapable of acting or helping. Consider this:

> To whom will you liken me and make me equal, and compare me, that we may be alike? Those who lavish gold from the purse, and weigh out silver in the scales, hire a goldsmith, and he makes it into a god; then they fall down and worship! They lift it upon their shoulders, they carry it, they set it in its place, and it stands; it cannot move from its place. If one cries to it, it does not answer or save him from his trouble (Isaiah 46:5-7).

Indeed, no one else/nothing else is worthy as our God. No one else/nothing else is able to know our needs and bring strength, guidance, and help into play. This is true even of the modern-day gods of possessions, prominence, popularity, pleasure, and portfolios.

As we seek to arrive at the heart of worship and the joy that results, our approach for the rest of this chapter will be to examine the word *PRAISE* and to use each of the six letters as a guide to understanding and entering wholeheartedly into worship. Knowing and practicing these six simple ideas will, I trust, pave the way to genuine and joyful worship in our own experience.

Most or all of us can probably guess what the "P" stands for in our *PRAISE* acronym (it's almost like asking who is buried in Grant's tomb). Yes, the "P" stands for *Praise* itself. The Bible is filled with encouragement to praise God and exalt His holy name:

> I will extol the LORD at all times; his praise will always be on my lips. My soul will boast in the LORD; let the afflicted hear and rejoice. Glorify the LORD with me; let us exalt his name together (Ps. 34:1-3).

> Shout with joy to God, all the earth! Sing the glory of his name, make his praise glorious! Say to God, "How awesome are your deeds! So great is your power that your enemies cringe before you. All the earth bows down to you; they sing praise to you, they sing praise to your name" (Ps. 66:1-4).

> Enter his gates with thanksgiving and his courts with praise; give thanks to him and praise his name. For the LORD is good and his love endures forever; his faithfulness continues through all generations (Ps. 100:4-5).

> Praise the LORD. Sing to the LORD a new song, his praise in the assembly of saints (Ps. 149:1).

> Praise the LORD. Praise God in his sanctuary; praise him in his mighty heavens. Praise him for his acts of power; praise him for his surpassing greatness. Praise him with the sounding of trumpet, praise him with the harp and lyre, praise him with tambourine and dancing, praise him with the strings and flute, praise him with the clash of cymbals, praise him with resounding cymbals. Let everything that has breath praise the LORD. Praise the LORD (Ps. 150:1-6).

> Through Jesus, therefore, let us continually offer to God a sacrifice of praise – the fruit of lips that confess his name (Hebrews 13:15).

According to these verses, our praise of the Lord should not be limited to the times when we are involved in group worship or worship on the Lord's Day, but praise is certainly a mainstay of what this worship is all about. Linked with the ideas of "merit" and "worth," praise involves expressing esteem of a person for his/her virtues and accomplishments. With this thought in mind, there is good reason for everything with breath to praise the Lord because His virtues and accomplishments are so amazing, so above and beyond anyone/anything else we encounter in the human realm.

We don't have to think very long and hard to come up with an extended list of God's virtues. God is holy and righteous, faithful and steadfast, compassionate and concerned, full of mercy and forgiveness, approachable and available, kind and good, gracious and giving, loving and impartial, selfless and pure, respectful of our free will and trustworthy, and always the same. His mind-boggling accomplishments include (just to name a few): the creation of the world and oversight of all things, the deliverance of His people in times of trouble and providing for all needs, devising and implementing the plan of salvation that culminates in victory over sin and death. Indeed,

"What god is so great as our God?" (Ps. 77:13b).

Singing and expressing praise to God for all of this has this great advantage, viz., that it draws the focus away from ourselves (our stresses and issues, our activities and challenges, our weaknesses and limited resources in the face of life's demands) and zeroes in on the greatness and power of God. Recently, I was reading in Ephesians and these words struck me:

> I pray also that the eyes of your heart may be enlightened in order that you may know the hope to which he has called you, the riches of his glorious inheritance in the saints, and his incomparably great power for us who believe. That power is like the working of his mighty strength, which he exerted in Christ when he raised him from the dead and seated him at his right hand in the heavenly realms, far above all rule and authority, power and dominion, and every title that can be given, not only in the present age but also in the one to come (Eph. 1:18-21, NKJV).

Here, Paul reminds us of "hope" (always a great asset for living in a fallen world, for without it we lapse into aimlessness and despair), of "a glorious inheritance," and of "his incomparably great power for us who believe." This power, the same power that raised Christ from the dead and exalted Him far above anyone/anything else that you can name, is the power that believers have available for daily living and for dealing with whatever comes our way. If you don't have goose bumps yet, you should, because this launches our lives into an extraordinary dimension that marvelously exceeds living merely on a human level with only human ingenuity and strength. As we worship and *praise* God for His virtues, accomplishments, and presence and power in our daily lives, joy will, without question, result.

The "R" in our *PRAISE* acronym stands for *Remember*. The

encouragement to remember and acts of remembering are interwoven throughout the Scriptures. Perhaps we are familiar with the following:

> Remember the Sabbath day by keeping it holy (Ex. 20:8).

> Remember that you were slaves in Egypt and that the LORD your God brought you out of there with a mighty hand and an outstretched arm. Therefore, the LORD your God has commanded you to observe the Sabbath day (Deut. 5:15).

> I will remember the deeds of the LORD; yes, I will remember your miracles of long ago. I will meditate on all your works and consider all your mighty deeds (Ps. 77:11-12).

> Remember your Creator in the days of your youth. . . (Eccl. 12:1a).

> Remember Lot's wife! (Luke 17:32).

> Remember Jesus Christ, raised from the dead, descended from David. This is my Gospel, for which I am suffering even to the point of being chained like a criminal. But God's word is not chained (2 Tim. 2:8-9).

There are numerous implications for worship interspersed among these verses, viz., that God's will is for us to observe a day of rest and worship and that the corporate memory of God's people continually emphasizes the mighty deeds of the Lord, particularly the redemption and deliverance that God has provided. However, there is another verse that readily comes to mind when Christians think of worship and remembering – "And he took bread, gave thanks and broke it, and gave it to them, saying, 'This is my body given for you; do this in remembrance of me,'" (Luke 22:19).

As Jesus and the disciples observe the Passover meal and remember the deliverance from Egyptian bondage, a new meal is established – the Lord's Supper. An even greater deliverance is about to be accomplished on the cross, but the reason for remembering remains the same. "Such recalling solidifies a community's identity by taking them back to their roots, to events that forged who they have now become. It gives them a chance, as one body, to reaffirm what God has done for them."[10] What is the Church all about? What makes the Body of Christ different from other groups? What makes the Body of Christ distinct and unique? Those questions are answered by remembering our roots and how we, as His Body, came to be. And, we continue to be true and faithful and united by remembering that we are not our own but have been bought with a price, the precious blood of our Lord and Savior (see 1 Cor. 6:19-20).

This remembering of Christ in the Lord's Supper and of God's mighty acts throughout the worship experience becomes a *reconnection* – a time to recall and to join with Christ in mind, body, and spirit. It becomes a *reliving* – a time to experience again the immensity and the huge cost of what Christ did on Calvary. Likewise, it is a *rejoicing* – a time to reflect on the Body of Christ worldwide (we are joined by millions in upholding the name of the Lord) and on the fact that all things will be fulfilled when Christ comes again. Finally, such remembering is a *refocusing* – a time to think about the reality and importance of the spiritual realm and that our God whose power exceeds that of sin and death is with us always as an ever-present help. Thus, oddly enough, our remembering is not something (as we might assume) that pertains only to the past. Instead, it impacts our present in powerful ways as well and looks forward to the future when God and Christ will ultimately triumph. Joyful worship is certainly about *remembering* – recapturing divine

---

10. Darrell L. Bock, *Luke: the NIV Application Commentary, from Biblical Text . . . to Contemporary Life*, the NIV Application Commentary Series, vol. 3, ed. Terry Muck, et al. (Grand Rapids, MI: Zondervan Publishing House, 1996), 551.

history and basking in its living implications for our present and our future.

Moving on to the "A" in our acronym of *PRAISE*, *Anticipation* is another element that leads to joy in worship. The author Robert Louis Stevenson presumably once said that he went to church on a particular Sunday and "was not depressed," implying that his usual experience was just the opposite. What about us, especially in the realm of anticipation? Do we look forward to the time of public worship? Do we anticipate that it is going to be a positive, inspiring, "well worth the effort" investment of our time? Or, do we regard worship merely as a duty to fulfill and believe that not much is likely to happen? The real goal is to get through the experience and to get on to the rest of the activities of the day. If this represents our thought process, our anticipation level will, no doubt, measure on the low to nonexistent side.

What a difference it would make if we were truly excited about going to worship. What if we woke up with the attitude, "Today, I'm going to encounter the divine in a special way. Today, I'm going to interact with God and Christ in ways that I don't typically do on the other days of the week. I expect the singing and special music to be uplifting. I expect the prayers to be vital in glorifying God and in expressing the needs of His people and His world in these stressed-out times. I expect, in some way, to meet God and Christ in observing the Lord's Supper and to be renewed in my spirit. I expect to come face to face with Him through the preaching of the Word, which will impact the way I think and act in the new week. I expect the fellowship to be warm and invigorating. I expect to enthusiastically praise His name so that His name is honored and glorified. In short, I expect that things will happen in worship that have no possibility of happening anywhere else, and that God will be pleased and I will go on my way rejoicing."

Such an approach may be a tall order if we have never looked at worship in this way, but anticipating this kind of experience will pave the way for the

Spirit to move in our hearts and minds as never before. Even if the humanly conducted service doesn't always "hit on all cylinders" in our mind, we will be much better off when *anticipation* is an integral part of our pre-worship thinking; when we believe that something out of the ordinary, something extraordinary is about to take to place.

The "I" in our formula for worship represents *Involvement*. This may be a new concept for us as well if we have been more into the "spectator" approach to worship hinted at above. "You really mean that I'm supposed to actively participate and to contribute to the worship experience, not just absorb things and wait for the worship leaders, the musicians, etc., to move me?" Yes, this is exactly what we're talking about. Many of the verses referred to throughout this chapter indicate that worshipers are very active and energetically involved when it comes to an authentic, biblical worship experience.

The old saying that "we get out of something what we put into it" comes to mind at this point. Putting very little into worship typically results in getting very little out of it, and it certainly falls flat in honoring, glorifying, and giving to God. So, what might involvement in worship look like? There are both public and private, outward and inward possibilities.

Depending on the church that you attend, you might have the opportunity to read Scripture or serve as a liturgist in some capacity. In some traditions, there are opportunities to pray publicly or perhaps to testify about the Lord's goodness or to request prayer for a particular need. There might be an encouragement to lift up holy hands in praise. Congregational singing will provide an outlet for exalting God and remembering some of the grand themes of the faith (keep in mind that congregational singing is not reserved for trained voices but is a vehicle for all of God's people to "make a joyful noise"). We can also participate when the offering plate is passed.

An attitude adjustment may be helpful here as well. Instead of thinking "here comes another call for my money – let's get this necessary but totally joyless time over with," what if we thought, "I wonder when they're going to have the offering. I can't wait for this moment of worship so that I can be a part of ensuring that Christ's church continues to be a beacon in my community, so that I can help in spreading the Gospel through my gift, and so that I can have a hand in assisting the poor and the disadvantaged who are so precious to Christ." Such an attitude, if needed, would surely transform this part of the service. Have you heard about the woman who fainted in church one Sunday morning and hit her head on the pew as she toppled over. An EMT who was present called for an ambulance. After getting her on the stretcher, the lady regained consciousness and motioned for her daughter to come near. The daughter leaned in close to hear what her mother wanted to say. "My offering is in my purse," she whispered. Here was someone who surely was a "cheerful giver" (see 2 Cor. 9:7) and didn't want to miss the opportunity to be involved in the offering. For her, it was a moment of significance.

These items represent the more public, outward involvement in worship. Other, inward expressions of involvement can be happening as well. We can enter into pre-worship prayer that God the Father, God the Son, and God the Holy Spirit will be uplifted and that both we and others will be drawn closer to Him. We can pray throughout the service for the music people that are involved that day. Likewise, we can pray that the preacher will be used of God for His purposes. Realizing that the message is "living water" from the Savior (although it comes through a human messenger), we can pray that our focus remains steadfast and free from distraction. Additionally, we can take in such items as symbols and banners that are displayed throughout the sanctuary and meditate on their significance. Basically, we are involved in worship by being spiritually "plugged in" and participating in all that is going on around us, not by simply being there and relying on our mere physical presence to be a sufficient offering to God. As we do, God will be uplifted, our worship will be a genuine offering to Him, and we, in turn, will be spiritually enriched.

Let us allow the "S" in our acronym to stand for *Service*. We have not always connected *worship* and *service* together. Perhaps you have had the experience, like me, of going to church and either reading in the bulletin or hearing the phrase, "Enter to Worship, Depart to Serve." This saying seemed appropriate in sending worshipers on their way but also tended to indicate that worship ends with the last "amen" of a corporate service and that *worship* and *service* are separate entities. Now, however, our thinking has begun to shift. At one of the churches where we worshipped, the closing charge was, "As our worship continues, our service has just begun." In short, this revised charge recognizes that corporate worship and service are inseparable (the one paves the way for the other) and that our worship doesn't end at the church doors but overflows into the highways and byways of our everyday lives.

The *Holman Illustrated Bible Dictionary* points out the following: "Worship may be understood in either a broad or narrow context. In a broad sense, worship is seen as a way of life (Rom.12:1). In this context all of life is viewed as an act of worship or service before God (1 Cor. 10:31; Col. 3:17)."[11] In this sense, our worship does, indeed, continue when we leave the physical church property. Our gathered worship prepares us to press on with our praise, thanksgiving, obedience, and service to God throughout the course of our daily activities. In the broad sense, according to Romans 12:1, this is worship, too.

As we may recall, Romans 12:1 encourages us "to offer your bodies as living sacrifices, holy and pleasing to God – which is your spiritual worship." Unlike the Ancients who were caught up in animal sacrifices, we now, in

---

11. Brand and Mitchell, *Holman Illustrated Bible Dictionary,* 1671.

Christ, offer ourselves as "living sacrifices" which, for Paul, constitutes worship. Thus, worship occurs when the body of Christ gathers to praise the Lord, to offer up prayers of thanksgiving and intercession, to hear the Word proclaimed, etc. (and is not to be neglected by rationalizing that "I'll just focus on the broader sphere of worship"), and it keeps on occurring every hour of every day.

Douglas Moo identifies, on a practical level, what some of this ongoing worship, outside the bounds of our corporate worship, looks like:

> As we eat our food, we worship God by thanking him for what he has given us, honoring him with our conversation, and providing for the bodies he has given us. As we sweat on the treadmill, we worship God by seeking to be good stewards of the body he has given us. As we seek (speaking for myself, sometimes in vain) to avoid driving with the same egotistic aggressiveness as others, we worship God by displaying the fruit of the Spirit. We do our work to the best of our ability, worshiping God by giving our best to our employers.[12]

Such offerings to God are added to the gifts of reaching out, sharing, and helping in His name. All of this drives home the fact that biblical worship is not limited to an hour or slightly more on any given Sunday. Corporate worship is extremely important as we publicly declare our allegiance to Christ and gather with the saints to glorify the Triune God. However, worship is not something that we "step out of" when we return home for Sunday dinner. Our public worship informs us, enriches us, and motivates us to continue in

---

12. Douglas J. Moo, *Romans: the NIV Application Commentary, from Biblical Text . . . to Contemporary Life*, the NIV Application Commentary Series, vol. 6, ed. Terry Muck, et al. (Grand Rapids, MI: Zondervan Publishing House, 2000), 397.

a spirit of worship when we're at work on Monday, cheering at a ball game on Thursday, or paying the bills on Saturday (thankfulness for the means to pay those bills is an act of worship). Thus, *worship* and *service* are definitely interrelated. There is joy when we maintain the link between the two for the combination of corporate and continuous worship honors Him thoroughly and keeps us close to the heart of God.

The final letter in our *PRAISE* acronym for worship stands for *Elevate*. This principle represents the thrust of all that we have been talking about. What we are trying to accomplish in worship, both public and personal, is to *elevate*, lift up God for who He is, what He has done, and what He continues to do through His power and the power of Christ and the Holy Spirit. Furthermore, we seek to *elevate* God before the world so that men and women are able to see and know God as Creator, Sustainer, Redeemer, and Friend. Fullness of life does not come by attaching ourselves to the pill-popping parties, the power-seeking personalities, or the pleasure-promising possibilities that surround us in popular culture. Instead, fullness of life comes by attaching ourselves to God and elevating His name, mercies and salvation, wisdom and ways in our journey through life. As we do so, we are elevated, ourselves, to a level of living above the temporary and above the reliance on human voices, speculations, and inventions, that being human have a built-in flaw factor. We are elevated to a level of life where we are loved, nurtured and cared for, and guided by the divine.

Several years ago, a minister friend told of leading Sunday worship and greeting the people after the service. One person, as he came through the line, felt compelled to relay his rather negative impressions of the service. "That was the worst worship service I have ever attended," he forcefully declared. Naturally, my friend was totally surprised and taken aback; maybe a few things could have gone a little better but he had no clue as to why someone would believe it was the worst service he had ever experienced.

After recovering, my friend said, "I'm sorry to hear you say that. What made you feel that way about the service?" The man replied, "You didn't sing the doxology!" It so happened that the disgruntled worshiper was a visitor so, at least, my friend didn't have to hear that every week after trying to do his best.

In reality, there is no mandated order of service for Christian worship. There is some precedence through the Christian centuries that certain elements be included in what the Church does when it gathers to exalt God, Christ, and the Holy Spirit, e.g., the Service of the Word and the Service of the Table (the Lord's Supper), prayers and praise.[13] However, no set, unalterable plan of what to do when and where has ever been prescribed. This allows us to proceed in various creative and meaningful ways. As we do, the six principles based on our *PRAISE* acronym – *Praise, Remember, Anticipation, Involvement, Service, and Elevation* – will surely be a source of great joy in our worship of the Holy One.

---

13. See Robert E. Webber, ed., *The Biblical Foundations of Christian Worship*, vol. 1, 103.

THE JOY OF PRAYER

"When she recognized Peter's voice, she was so overjoyed
she ran back without opening it and exclaimed,
'Peter is at the door.'"

Acts 12:4

The following story always causes me to smile. It centers on four-year-old Bobby who was about to have a new brother or sister. His mother told him that a new little one would arrive in several months, and she asked him to pray that everything would go well and that the new baby would be healthy. Bobby began with good intentions and prayed faithfully for a couple of weeks. However, as sometimes happens with the very young (and sometimes with those of us who are a little bit older as well), Bobby's attentiveness to his prayers began to wane, and he soon forgot to pray for his mother and the new baby. The big day arrived and, to Bobby's surprise, he learned that he had not one, but two baby sisters. When he was finally able to see his mother, she said, "Bobby, aren't you glad that you prayed for your new baby sisters?" "Oh, yes," he replied, "but aren't you glad that I stopped praying when I did!"

I think we can understand Bobby's four-year-old point of view but, of course, there are never times when we should stop praying. The *Parable of the Persistent Widow* is introduced with these words, "Then Jesus told his disciples a parable to show them that they should always pray and not give up" (Luke 18:1). There are numerous reasons as to why we should always pray and several of them come to light in this passage from Acts 12 that records a powerful example of prayer in the life of Peter and the early Church. I believe that the reasons given here for continually praying and others that are provided throughout the Scriptures lead to joy in prayer.

In Acts 12, Peter is in prison. Recently, Herod "had James, the brother of John, put to death with the sword" (verse 2). This, apparently, pleased some of the people so Herod is now pursuing a similar course with Peter in order to further enhance his popularity with his subjects. This situation, however, will have a different outcome and prayer figures prominently in what takes place. Thus, the passage reveals several key factors as to why prayer is so important and why it can be the source of much joy in our lives.

First of all, let us consider this: there is joy in prayer because *Prayer is a Sustaining Force*. Indeed, prayer brings the resources of God into play in our lives with the result that we have His sustaining presence and strength through whatever situations and challenges arise in our earthly lives.

Prayer is certainly a *Sustaining Force* here in the life of Peter. Verse 5 is central to our thoughts – "So Peter was kept in prison, but the church was earnestly praying to God for him." Lots of prayers were being offered up on Peter's behalf (this is emphasized again in verse 12). Consequently, Peter was able to take this situation in stride because of the sustaining power of God.

We may hurry over what is happening here, but we need to realize that this is a pretty bleak time for Peter. As indicated above, Herod seems intent on pursuing the same outcome in Peter's case as he had just carried out with

James. So, Peter is basically on death row. According to verse 6, it is the night before he goes to trial. Therefore, if Herod has his way, Peter's days are pretty limited. "Four squads of four soldiers each" are assigned to guard Peter, so any thought of escape is definitely far-fetched. However, notice what Peter is doing the night before all of this comes to pass – *he's sleeping.* I would contend that he's able to sleep because of the sustaining power of God. Tomorrow doesn't appear very promising. It could be his last or one of his last days on earth, but he knows that whatever tomorrow brings it will also bring God and all of God's concern, resources, and promises. Peter still lives in the confidence that he will be in God's care regardless of what the circumstances around him happen to be and regardless of how they turn out in the end.

From our life in the military, I think Judy and I can also testify to the sustaining power of prayer. As you probably know, the military life usually includes times of separation and being apart. Over our long career, I figure that the two of us were separated between three and a half and four years. I don't say that to elicit any sympathy or to hold up what we did; that's kind of how it works in the military. Actually, we were very fortunate. Many others have done far more, but God always sustained us and brought us back together. Not that it was easy, but we were able to press on in His strength and presence.

I remember my first extended deployment. I was in the Navy for less than a year when my ship headed over to the Western Pacific for a six month "cruise," as we say. And I remember thinking a couple of times, "What in the world am I doing here? A year ago, I was in a beautiful part of Indiana. Life was good. Judy and the kids were close by. Things were going well at the church. Now, I'm over here 12,000 miles from home with four more months to go before I get back. What in the world was I thinking when I signed up to do this?"

But, over the years, we always felt that the military chaplaincy was where God wanted us to be. We believed that we were providing effective ministry in that setting, and we learned that God was always with us and would bring us through. This belief and bringing the resources of the Lord into play through prayer always provided an underlying confidence and joy. It wasn't always in the exuberant sense, not that every day was a "smiley face" day, but that our lives were always enveloped and guided by the divine. Our experience has been that there is joy in prayer because *Prayer is a Sustaining Force.*

Prayer can also be a Protecting Force. Here we have to be a little careful. We do not understand everything that happens or all of the workings of God. We certainly cannot explain everything that takes place, even for Christians and people of faith. At times, we would like to make our faith into a big vending machine whereby we pray, push the selection we want, and things come out according to what we prefer and have ordered. But it doesn't quite work this way. We must remember that while Peter was rescued, James was not. When tragedies occur, such as a plane crash or a mass shooting and many people are either killed or injured, there are bound to be people of faith involved, and we are at a loss to answer the nagging question of "why." Thus, I believe that the following comments are very informative at this point:

> What is common to these situations is that both Peter and James were faithful to Christ. Just as the disciples earnestly prayed for Peter's release (v. 5), we too have the freedom to pray earnestly for physical deliverance. But we must leave it to God to let his sovereignty over a situation be expressed in the way he regards best. What is most important is that, like James and Peter, we remain faithful and obedient to God regardless of the outcome of a crisis we face.[14]

14. Ajith Fernando, *Acts: the NIV Application Commentary, from Biblical Text . . . to Contemporary Life*, the NIV Application Commentary Series, vol. 5, ed. Terry Much, et al. (Grand Rapids, MI: Zondervan Publishing House, 1998), 364.

So, we have to be careful of our expectations of *Prayer as a Protecting Force*. However, I believe with Theodore Ferris that at least two things happen when we pray. One, we are drawn closer to God, and, two, some things happen that would not otherwise happen when we employ the power and the resource of prayer.[15]

Fortunately for him, Peter experienced prayer as a protecting force. Notice verse 7 – "Suddenly an angel of the Lord appeared and a light shone in the cell. He struck Peter on the side and woke him up. 'Quick, get up!' he said, and the chains fell off Peter's wrists." Then, the angel led him past the guards and past the gate, out into the city, and out of harm's way.

Here we have a rather dramatic example of prayer as a protecting force. Remember, the church was still praying. And, while it may not always happen in such a spectacular fashion, I believe that God and Christ still watch over their people today. The Psalmist said, "The angel of the LORD encamps around those who fear him, and he delivers them" (Ps. 34:7). Furthermore, I believe that Judy and I have been the beneficiaries of such divine concern.

We did a lot of praying during our tour in Sicily. Overall, it was a great tour. We got to do quite a bit of traveling throughout Europe and live in a different culture, which was so interesting and fascinating. However, we were also there in the mid-1980s when Omar Khaddafy was rattling around. Libya was only an hour away by air, and there were threats against the base and the Commanding Officer and his family during this time. I remember especially the situation for Sunday night youth group. The Commanding Officer's daughter attended and, when she came to participate, the Marines came along for protection. So, we would send James and Christine off to youth group where the Marines were standing by with M-16 rifles. I doubt if very many of us have sent our kids off to youth group where the U. S.

---

15. Theodore P. Ferris, "The Acts of the Apostles: Exposition," in *The Interpreter's Bible*, vol. 9, ed. George A. Buttrick, et al. (New York and Nashville: Abingdon Press, 1954), 158.

Marines had to be present to ensure safety. Obviously, we felt things were pretty much under control, otherwise, we would have canceled the meetings. But, we prayed, and the Lord saw us through.

Here's a different kind of situation. While we were in Connecticut, Judy had a medical episode. Unfortunately, a blood vessel leaked in the back of her head and caused a lot of havoc. The symptoms were similar to a stroke or an aneurism, but the good part is that after things were taken care of medically and after about six months of fully regaining her strength, there are no lingering effects. To our knowledge, her recovery is complete, and it should not happen again.

My reason for mentioning this is that this could have happened anywhere or at any time. She could have been alone. She could have been driving and driven off the road. It happened in winter when there was snow and ice on the roads. But guess where we were when this episode took place? We were attending what we call in the Navy a "Hail and Farewell" which is a get-together to welcome newcomers to the command and to say goodbye to those who are leaving. Our staff was gathered for this occasion and, when this came upon Judy, there were two doctors and two nurses in the house. If you're going to have some kind of medical situation, what more could you ask for? As I mentioned, Judy could have been alone or just with me. Hopefully, I would have helped but who knows if I would have done the right things. These good folks stabilized Judy, called for an ambulance and got her to the hospital, and things, though a challenge, worked out. Some might say that this was merely a coincidence. I believe, however, that since we were walking with the Lord and praying as we went that the Lord intervened in this wonderful way. Things happen that otherwise might not happen when we pray.

Let's consider one other item, different from the above, about this matter of *Prayer as a Protecting Force*. As already stated, prayer brings us closer to God. As we pray and live in the Lord, we live more in line with the ways and will of God. By so doing, we walk in right and good paths and, thus, we avoid many of the pitfalls of life. We end up in healthy and beneficial situations. We tend not to walk in our own ways or the ways of the world which are often a recipe for reaping disaster or trying developments. Our lives are better and less complicated.

The reality is that, as humans, we are not going to avoid all mistakes in our lives. We will probably have some lapses in judgment along the way, typically when we lean on our own understanding (see Proverbs 3:5-8). However, prayer can be a protective force, both in the sense that some things will happen that otherwise would not happen and in the sense that, by drawing closer to God, we end up in places that are far better for us. We end up with a lifestyle that avoids so many problems and difficulties that might otherwise beset us. In this, I believe, there is great joy.

Another cause for joy in prayer is because *Prayer is a Multiplying Force.* In short, our own human strength, human wisdom, and human resources are limited. As we have mentioned before, there are times when we need strength and wisdom and resources beyond what we can conjure up on our own. Life, sometimes, is just too demanding. It takes unexpected twists and turns; it takes twists and turns that can throw us off-guard and leave us wondering what we should do and how we will be able to make it through. It's true for all of us. One month, everything can be clicking on all cylinders. The next month you can be mourning the loss of a dear loved one or close friend. For military people, one month you can be enjoying the beautiful fall foliage of New England or some other locale. The next month you can be in the midst of armed conflict in a combat zone. Through prayer, we multiply our strength, wisdom, and resources because we involve God, the great Lord of all things. Wherever we go and whatever we experience, we know that God is already there before us, to be with us and strengthen us.

The Scriptures are full of examples where prayer is employed as a multiplying force. We may be quite familiar with some (e.g., Daniel in the lion's den); others may not come readily to mind. In 2 Chronicles 32, we have an example that may fall into the less familiar category (these events are also recorded in 2 Kings 18-19 and Isaiah 36-37). Near the end of the eighth century BCE, King Sennacherib of Assyria is intent on overrunning Judah. Although greatly over-matched, King Hezekiah encourages his people with these words:

> Be strong and courageous. Do not be afraid or discouraged because of the king of Assyria and the vast army with him, for there is a greater power with us than with him. With him is only the arm of flesh, but with us is the LORD our God to help us and to fight our battles (vss. 7-8).

This wonderful insight gave the people confidence in the face of their outward circumstances, but it turned Sennacherib into a boaster and a blasphemer. Upon hearing of Judah's refusal to surrender, he sent a message saying in essence, "You people are very misguided. Come to your senses. I have conquered greater lands than you and, in each case, their people trusted in their gods but the outcome was always the same – I prevailed! Don't make the same foolish mistake."

Some of Sennacherib's comments and those of his cohorts got pretty nasty as is seen in verses 15 and 18-19:

> Now do not let Hezekiah deceive you and mislead you like this. Do not believe him, for no god of any nation or kingdom has been able to deliver his people from my hand or the hand of my fathers. How much less will your god deliver you from my hand!

> Then they called out in Hebrew to the people of Jerusalem who were on the wall, to terrify them and make them afraid in order to capture the city. They spoke about the God of Jerusalem as they did about the gods of the other peoples of the world – the work of men's hands.

This is all intimidating stuff. The mighty Assyrians are at the gates and Sennacherib is saying, "No one else with their gods has stood up to me; your puny nation with your lightweight, insignificant god won't do any better, even worse." His men reiterate the same message, claiming that the God of Judah is just like the others who have been fashioned with human hands.

What else could Hezekiah do but pray: "King Hezekiah and the prophet Isaiah son of Amoz cried out in prayer to heaven about this" (vs. 20). The result – the true God sent an angel to deliver His people and sent Sennacherib scurrying. Obviously, it was Sennacherib who was misguided about the power and ability of Judah's God.

Often our response to such a powerful example of *Prayer as a Multiplying Force* is to think that this was for a particular time and place, and it's just too much to believe that prayer could bring about such results in our own experience. When these thoughts arise, I always like to recall what James stated in 5:17-18: "Elijah was a man just like us. He prayed earnestly that it would not rain, and it did not rain on the land for three and a half years. Again he prayed, and the heavens gave rain, and the earth produced its crops." Remember, too, that these words come immediately after one of the most beloved verses about prayer in all of Scripture – "The prayer of a righteous man is powerful and effective."

Certainly, prayer is a multiplying force and people just like us have prayed and discovered this reality to be true. What we need to keep in mind is that God "is able to do immeasurably more than all we ask or imagine, according to his power that is at work within us" (Eph. 3:20).

Likewise, we need to remember with Hezekiah that there is far greater power with us than with anything that we might face in this world. With this perspective, joy is our constant companion.

Our final thought about joy and prayer in Acts 12 is the thread that runs throughout these verses we have been considering – *Prayer is a Collective Force*. Prayer is an individual spiritual discipline that keeps us in close contact with God and His power, and it plays a major role in helping us to remain spiritually focused in the flow of life. However, prayer is also a force to be utilized and engaged in by the Church as a whole, multiplying our efforts and demonstrating to God our seriousness and unity regarding the matters that we are praying about.

In other places in Acts, Luke emphasizes that the first century Church was a praying church. "They all joined together constantly in prayer. . ." (1:14); and "they devoted themselves to the apostles' teaching and to the fellowship, to the breaking of bread and to prayer" (2:42). While in prison in Rome, Paul encouraged the Church to pray on his behalf, stating "for I know that through your prayers and the help given by the Spirit of Jesus Christ, what has happened to me will turn out for my deliverance" (Phil. 1:19). A beautiful thought occurs in 2 Cor. 1:11a where, after speaking of the hardships on some of his travels and even despairing of life, Paul says that he and his colleagues continue to trust in the deliverance of God "as you help us by your prayers." Paul and the early Church definitely believed in the power that is unleashed when God's people join together as a community to make heaven aware of our unified concerns.

Just as there is joy in our personal prayer life, joy also results when we join with others to pray for needs and situations. Individually and collectively, our prayers help to advance the Kingdom. They help to raise up "workers for the harvest field" (Matt. 9:38 and Luke10:2). They may help to see someone through a particularly difficult time, perhaps paving the way for a reconciliation or for someone to move from an unemployed status to the ranks of the employed. Perhaps our efforts assist someone through a serious operation or illness with results that defy explanation unless we include the hand of God in the process. Joy comes when we know that we are contributing to the spiritual work of the Kingdom, and when we see God at work in the prayers of His people.

Having said all of this, it is important to emphasize that we must also believe in the power of prayer. This may seem like an odd comment at the end of a chapter that is all about the efficacy of prayer and the joy that we can experience as a result of communicating with God, either personally or as a community. However, the body of believers here in Acts 12 stumbled at this very point, and so may we. In the verse that headlined this chapter, Rhoda was "overjoyed" because their prayers had been answered – Peter was knocking at the door! But did the others share her joy? Hardly – they thought she had lost it, that she was out of her mind. If psychologists had been around in the first century, Rhoda would have been sent off for a psychological evaluation!

It is interesting that "while the big iron gate of the prison opened with no effort to let Peter out (vs. 10), he was unable to get past the gate of his own friend's house."[16] This "surely it can't be true" response is also curious since Peter had already experienced a miraculous release from prison on an earlier occasion (Acts 5:19-20). Apparently, those gathered for prayer had some preconceived notions about what prayer could and couldn't do, and they were just not able to conceive of such a bold answer to their intercessions. Or, in their defense, maybe they were merely praying that Peter would remain faithful through what was happening ("faithful issues" had come up before

---

16. Fernando, *Acts*, 363.

for Peter); therefore, they were totally surprised when God chose to work in such a dramatic fashion. Whatever was going on, we should never limit God or be surprised at what He can and will do.

This story circulated a few years ago. When a nightclub opened on Main Street in a small town, the only church in town organized an all-night prayer meeting. The members asked God to burn down the club. Within a few minutes, lightning struck the club, and it burned to the ground. The owner sued the church, which denied responsibility. After hearing from both sides, the judge said, "It seems that wherever the guilt may lie, the nightclub owner believes in prayer, while the church does not."

I trust that individually and collectively we believe in prayer. We need to because it is "powerful and effective." It is also a great source of joy because it is a *Sustaining Force*, it can be a *Protective Force*, it is a *Multiplying Force*, and it is a *Collective Force* that enriches us and unleashes incredible power in our lives and in the life of Christ's body, the Church.

THE JOY AMIDST TRIALS

"Consider it pure joy, my brothers, whenever you
face trials of many kinds, because you know that the
testing of your faith develops perseverance."

James 1:2-3

One bright, sunny weekend, Judy and I took off on a day trip to visit a tourist town in northwest Connecticut. We went to enjoy the day and the scenery, and to stop at a Belgian chocolate shop located in the town. You can't go wrong with Belgian chocolate.

After getting our supply of chocolate, we wandered through the other shops. One of them had an assortment of plaques with pithy sayings. I moved away after being amused by some of the quips. Then, two women began to survey the display I had just left. I really wasn't trying to eavesdrop, but the shop was small and I was close enough to overhear their conversation.

I don't remember the exact saying one of them was commenting on, but it was some variation of the adage "when life gives you lemons, make lemonade." In this woman's opinion, the person who came up with this thought should be ashamed. Life isn't that simple, she indicated, and it's better to be more realistic and not so naïve when it comes to managing the demands that life sometimes throws at us. I guess she would line up more with "the glass is half-empty" approach when faced with any trial or difficulty.

No doubt, this person is not alone in her outlook because life does become problematic at times, and we find ourselves dealing with matters that are far from what we desire. One of the *Peanuts* cartoons illustrates this very vividly. Linus and Charlie Brown are talking and Linus says, "Sometimes I feel that life has passed me by. . .". The next frame shows the two of them in deep thought while Linus mutters a big "Sigh." He then turns to Charlie Brown and asks, "Do you ever feel that way, Charlie Brown?" He replies, "No, I feel it has knocked me down and walked all over me!" As the saying goes, "I guess you'll have that."

The person I overheard in the tourist shop would probably conclude that I, too, should be ashamed of myself for suggesting that there can be "joy amidst trials." Trials are unwanted and can be inconvenient at the least and very painful at the most. At first, this appears to be an oxymoron; the two words "joy" and "trials" just don't belong together (like the term "sweet and sour sauce" – how can you have it both ways at the same time?). However, the person of faith has to come to grips with this seemingly incongruous thought since it appears very conspicuously in the Scriptures, specifically here in the book of James. Without question, it is hard to connect "joy" and "trials" together, but, given what James says, there must be something to the idea that joy can be found even in the midst of trials.

Trials are difficulties, hardships, disappointments, struggles, and other negative challenges that confront us, and they most assuredly arise in the course of our lives. They arise from such things as:

> Growing up – trying to fit in, make the grade, and be accepted aren't always fun.

Poor decisions – getting involved with another person while married turns out not to be as attractive as it seemed at first and can have serious consequences.

The nature of the world – germs that cause illness circulate around us and gravity is always in play (meaning, that gravity is usually our friend but if your plane has just taken off and malfunctions, it is not your friend).

Greed, selfishness, and stubbornness (both our own and that of others) – someone maneuvers questionably to get the promotion instead of us. Or, we always have to have our way; thus, we reap conflict since we hardly ever consider the needs or wishes of others and what they have to say.

Being in the wrong place at the wrong time – try not to do your banking when a robber might come in and start shooting (you might want to avoid Fridays since, according to The Book of Useless Information, fifty percent of bank robberies take place on the sixth day of the week).

Not paying attention – be careful of eating, reading, putting on makeup, and using a cell phone while driving. Also, don't become so busy that you fail to see family and close relationships slipping away.

Circumstances that develop in the flow of life – the paycheck doesn't stretch far enough, relationships break up, people disappoint us, children desire their freedom before they are ready to handle it, plans and goals are thwarted and fall by the wayside.

Our faith – Christians can be misunderstood, ridiculed, and even persecuted; or, our faith compels us to speak up when others are silent and would rather look the other way. Not everyone is enamored with our encouragement to live righteously.

In light of such realities, we can avoid some trials but not all. We can control some things by good living and good judgment, others we cannot. Sometimes, things just happen (like the downsizing of our employer, like a highly undesirable and devastating pandemic). Unless we're the luckiest person ever to walk the planet, we will experience trials at various points in our lives. They are part of the human experience.

Over the years, I have sometimes likened what happens to us to what happened to the car we took with us for our tour of duty in Sicily. The car, a four-door compact, was relatively blemish free when we left. It was, you might say, "battle-scarred" when we returned. Take a tour with me around the vehicle after it survived the Sicilian experience and a few months back in the States.

Originally, on the driver's side at the front, there was a rubber bumper guard attached to the front bumper that curved around the side for protection. One week after the car arrived in Sicily, one of us backed out of the driveway, caught this guard on the gate, and ripped it off. We never found a good way to reattach it.

Next, notice the headlight on the passenger's side – it is held in place with duct tape. Our best guess was that a neighborhood youngster came flying off a skateboard ramp and wiped out the plastic fixture that held it in place (it was hard to get replacement parts in Sicily). Every now and then, when the tape got old or the airflow tore at the tape, it would dangle out of its place and hang there by the wires attached to it. It resembled one of those eyeballs that you get at a novelty shop that is used to scare people, the ones that pop out of fake glasses and bounce up and down on a spring, looking grotesque. That was our headlight in its worst moments.

Now, follow the assorted scrapes and dents down the passenger's side, around the back of the car to the rear wheel wall on the driver's side where there is no paint. Here, one of us was backing out of the garage, turned too soon, and left the paint on the garage door. In this person's defense, it should be noted that Sicilian/Italian garages and driveways can be very narrow and this could happen to anyone.

Finally, come forward just a bit to the rear door on the driver's side where there is a crease that was not put there by the manufacturer. The crease represents the blending of two cars in our driveway; something that we didn't like to talk about very much at our house.

The point to all of this is that similar things happen in life. We would like for our lives to be like the pre-Sicily vehicle – unblemished without any nicks, marks, and scrapes. In reality, the longer we live the more our lives resemble the post-Sicily car – nicked and marked, scuffed up by driving up and down the roadways of life; scuffed up by the experiences and trials that we encounter. If we're fortunate, these nicks and marks are not major, and we shrug them off and go on. But, for some, major ones come along or the accumulation of the nicks and marks over the years begins to wear on us, and we may find ourselves losing some of our zest for life and even questioning God.

It goes without saying that a person needs to be spiritually minded and seeking God for the idea of "joy amidst trials" to make any sense. As we have seen, the worldly mind generally believes that the idea is bogus, unrealistic, and foreign to rational thought. On the other hand, the spiritual mind entertains the thought that there are some marvelous advantages to be gleaned from moving through trials in God's strength and not allowing them to make us bitter or pessimistic in our outlook. After all, we are still going to be here after most trials, and *we can either seek the joy that can be found in managing them or be miserable from the experience.* We do not have the luxury of trading in our lives for a new model as we do with a car when it becomes nicked and marked.

The big advantage given here in James for successfully managing trials is that *Trials Can Enhance Our Perseverance*. Again, as we saw with prayer in the last chapter, such perseverance can be both on an individual level as well as for the community of faith as a whole. The recipients of James' epistle are familiar with personal trials, with church-related trials (notice the discussion of "favoritism" in chapter two), and with church-targeted trials.

What James is saying is that joy comes when we claim to be a disciple of Christ and, by weathering trials, we prove to ourselves and to God that we are not just in it for the blessings and the "sunny skies" that many think must follow. When trials come for Christians just as they do for others, it is a time to persevere and prove our mettle. It is not a time to fold our tent and go elsewhere, but a time to build our character, our resilience, our dependability, and our track record of faithfulness. As we do, God is glorified and His Kingdom has the advantage of a staunch asset for His purposes. It is a time to move forward in maturity and spiritual growth.

Addressing trials specifically related to faith, Peter spoke of similar things when he encouraged his readers in this way:

> In this you greatly rejoice [our living hope and salvation], though now for a little while you have to suffer grief in all kinds of trials. These have come to you so that your faith – of greater worth than gold, which perishes even though refined by fire – may be proved genuine and may result in praise, glory and honor when Jesus Christ is revealed (1 Peter 1:6-7).

Just as fire refines gold and removes any impurities, so the "fire" of trials refines us (if handled properly), helps us to work out impurities and inconsistencies, and leaves us steadfast with a genuine faith devoted to God. As James says in 1:4, "Perseverance must finish its work so that you may be mature and complete, not lacking anything." Our goal is to keep striving toward a faith that is uncompromised, not littered with a host of eyebrow-raising, questionable tendencies that cause others to wonder, "How in the world does that fit in with Christianity?" Trials definitely help in this process.

In his book *1776* about the Revolutionary War, David McCullough quotes Colonel Henry Knox who said, "We want great men who, when fortune frowns, will not be discouraged."[17] God is looking for such men and women in the spiritual trenches today. His is looking for individuals who remain committed even when trials are the order of the day. It is possible to rise up and be these men and women when trials are viewed with the proper spiritual perspective.

Another important advantage that results when trials are managed successfully and a key to persevering is that *Trials Also Enhance Our Reliance*. We live in a culture that seeks "good times" and comfort and believes that anything less is unfair and not right. The government should step in and do something, or we ought to be able to sue someone if any kind of discomfort or difficulty is taking place. Consequently, in order to appropriately handle the trials that come, we need to be grounded in the mindset and strength of God, relying upon Him or trials will trip us up and leave us grumbling and discontent.

Trials and challenges should drive us to God for guidance and help. Fortunately, we are invited to seek and ask for these very things. Jesus said, "Come to me, all you who are weary and burdened, and I will give you rest" (Matt. 11:28). Have you ever paid attention to the scope of that invitation? – "all," anyone who is struggling or faced with a trial. And, since all are summoned, the logical conclusion is that it's not just the minor, lightweight

---

17. David McCullough, *1776* (New York: Simon & Schuster, 2005), 201.

matters that Christ can assist with, but it's anything that arises regardless of the degree of difficulty involved. Christ would not extend such an invitation only to say later, "Oh, I'm sorry, your need is too great. On a scale of 1 to 10, I only meant that you could come if your burden falls into the lower ranges of the scale, let's say from 1 to 5, not the higher ranges." Thanks be to God that no one has ever been treated in this way by our Lord.

We can also remember James' words in 1:5 at this point: "If any of you lacks wisdom, he should ask God, who gives generously to all without finding fault, and it will be given to him." Wisdom is a key commodity in all of this, but we may be reluctant to approach God about it if we think His response may be something like, "I suppose you can have it, but you should have known better in the first place," or "OK, but you sure waited long enough before you got around to asking." To the contrary, God grants wisdom without browbeating and finding fault. He wants us to be equipped so that we can be victorious in life. He offers us what we truly need in the midst of trials – Christ's presence and godly wisdom.

Arthur John Gossip was a noted British preacher in the first half of the twentieth century. He lost his dear wife suddenly at a relatively young age. The first sermon he preached after returning to the pulpit was entitled, "But When Life Tumbles In, What Then?" Here are just a few lines of what Gossip had to say:

> I do not understand this life of ours. But still less can I comprehend how people in trouble and loss and bereavement can fling away peevishly from the Christian faith. In God's name, fling to what? Have we not lost enough without losing that too? . . . You people in the sunshine may believe the faith, but we in the shadow must believe it. We have nothing else.[18]

---

18. Arthur John Gossip, *The Hero in Thy Soul: Being an Attempt to Face Life Gallantly* (Edinburgh: T. & T. Clark, 1928), 110-111.

Although I came across these words some time ago, Gossip's thought of "fling to what?" has lingered in my mind. There is no viable alternative; there is no other voice that has anything of consequence to say. Here was a man with a right to speak about trials and hardships, and he concluded that "the faith works, fulfills itself, is real; and that its most audacious promises are true."[19] He concluded that God will always sustain us as long we continue to rely upon His grace. Surely joy, i.e., ultimate joy, resides in these realities.

Still another advantage of successfully managing trials which leads to joy is that *Trials Enhance Our Usefulness*. Paul's words in 2 Corinthians 1:3-4 are most appropriate here: "Praise be to the God and Father of our Lord Jesus Christ, the Father of compassion and the God of all comfort, who comforts us in all our troubles, so that we can comfort those in any trouble with the comfort we ourselves have received from God."

Scott Hafemann points out that, in these verses, "Paul moves from a statement of who God *is* in verse 3, to a declaration of what God *does* in 4a, to God's *goal* for doing it in 4b."[20] God *is* the source of compassion and all comfort. God *does* comfort us in any and all troubles. God's *goal* is that Paul and others who benefit from this comfort will, in turn, comfort others in trouble by sharing the same grace and consolation. The flow of comfort to us is not intended to stop with our own peace and reassurance, but it is intended to keep flowing from us to others who are beset with trials and troubles. God's *goal* is that our usefulness is enhanced as we discover His marvelous, sustaining activity in the face of life's challenges.

I never looked forward to those times when I was going to deploy and be away from the family for six to seven months at a time. It was, however, part of the ministry that Judy and I had chosen and, having done

19. Ibid., 111.
20. Scott J. Hafemann, *2 Corinthians: the NIV Application Commentary, from Biblical Text . . . to Contemporary Life*, the NIV Application Commentary Series, vol. 8, ed. Terry Muck, et al. (Grand Rapids, MI: Zondervan Publishing House, 2000), 62.

it, it enabled me to assist and comfort others when it came their turn to experience the demands of separation. I have no clue as to how many times I have shared the grace of God for managing time apart from spouses and children. Having been through those demands, uplifted by the hand of God, I like to think that I had something worthwhile to say and share. I trust I was useful to God in doing so.

The same thing can be true of each one of us – we can be useful in helping someone else negotiate trying circumstances. Have we been through the loss of a job, a serious illness, the troubling loss of a relationship, challenges in raising children, the loss of a loved one, the death of a dream, "stabbed in the back" at work, passed over while someone less qualified received the promotion, or ridiculed or persecuted in some form for our faith? At the time, helping someone else through a similar time was far from our mind; now that time has passed and God has given us strength and wisdom to keep putting one foot in front of another, we realize that we can help to bear someone else's burden and help to ease the strain and pain they may be experiencing. Great satisfaction and fulfillment come with being useful to God and to others, even though we are not excited about our own original trial. Joy comes when we participate with the God of all comfort in doing what He does and carrying out His goals.

Finally, there is joy in successfully managing trials because *Trials Enhance Our Future*. Before wrapping up his thoughts on the subject of trials, James goes on to say, "Blessed is the man who perseveres under trial, because when he has stood the test, he will receive the crown of life that God has promised to those who love him" (1:12). Here, James brings together the things we have been talking about and reveals the bottom line, the sum total when they are all added up. James' addition looks like this:

Trials & Testing + Persevering & Passing the Test
= Blessedness & the Crown of Life

Just as $2 + 2 = 4$, so these elements added together always come out the same in this spiritual equation. The crown referred to is not a physical crown like the crown of olive or ivy branches that athletes of the time received for dedication, discipline, and excellence. It is not like the *Burger King* crown (not very desirable unless you're a kid or need something for a costume party) and not like one of the British royal crowns on display in the Tower of London (extremely desirable from a material point of view but lacking in any ultimate, eternal value). Instead, this crown is priceless. It is life itself; it is life with God, forever.

Other verses and passages hold up this same thought. One of the verses I memorized early on as a child was Revelation 2:10b – "Be faithful, even to the point of death, and I will give you the crown of life." In the Beatitudes, Jesus said, "Blessed are you when people insult you, persecute you and falsely say all kinds of evil against you because of me. Rejoice and be glad, because great is your reward in heaven, for in the same way they persecuted the prophets who were before you" (Matt. 5:11). Also, Peter weighs in once again in 1 Peter 4:12-13: "Dear friends, do not be surprised at the painful trial you are suffering, as though something strange were happening to you. But rejoice that you participate in the sufferings of Christ, so that you may be overjoyed when his glory is revealed."

Whether trials come as a result of our faith or whether they come because of stressful, demanding circumstances in living out our lives, we can look beyond the discomfort that is happening to us and realize that a lot more is going on and a lot more is at stake. Trials are not only about our distress or afflictions (although these can be very real and should not be minimized or taken lightly), but they are also about developing perseverance and faithfulness, about spiritual growth and formation, about reliance upon God and being useful to Him and to others, about sharing with Christ and advancing what He has set in motion, about exalting and glorifying our Lord and Savior, about testing and passing, and, in the end, about sharing in His life that continues when our earthly life has run its course.

Allow me to share two more items before closing this chapter. *ITEM NUMBER ONE* – Surely someone will bring up the pandemic of 2020 and ask if its challenges, changes, and trials don't undermine the main idea of this chapter. The pandemic does present its challenges, but I trust that not even it causes us to "fling away" from faith to something else.

The pandemic brought trials to new levels of intensity, to levels that many had not experienced before. The challenges and trials were not limited to the following but included: social distancing and social isolation; staying at home with everyone present all day; others living alone with reduced outside contact; struggling to pay the rent and other bills; reduction in work hours, reduction in pay, or having no job at all; wearing masks; changes in shopping and eating out routines; and the loss of loved ones and friends. One story in the *Wisconsin State Journal* newspaper of Madison, WI, told of a woman who lost fifteen family members and friends during the pandemic. "I don't know if I ever will . . . process all of them," said Kimberly Montgomery of Milwaukee, WI. "The shock factor, it never wears off. But it tempers."[21] Obviously, a person could be overwhelmed in the wake of such developments.

I don't want to come off as unsympathetic or just give some trite, religious cliché answer to the pain that so many experienced, but we have to find some way to keep moving forward or our lives will turn into one big pit of misery. Isaiah 40:31 may help at this point. This has been one of my favorite verses in the Bible for a long time, for it states: "But those who hope in the LORD will renew their strength. They will soar on wings like eagles; they will run and not grow weary, they will walk and not be faint."

---

21. Carrie Antlfinger, "15 Losses: COVID-19 Virus Claims 15 People in Life of One Woman," *Wisconsin State Journal*, March 14, 2021, B13.

I like to think that these words refer to three kinds of periods in our lives. Sometimes, something wonderful and exceptional is taking place. It may be a wedding, a graduation, a new job, a promotion, a college acceptance letter, a special anniversary. At such times, we are able to soar like eagles. There are other times when nothing out of the ordinary is going on, but things are generally going well with little stress to contend with. At these times, we are able to carry on in a good fashion, to run without becoming weary. Then, there are times when troubles come, trials mound up, and we find ourselves wondering which way to turn. Even then, we are able to "walk and not be faint." If we keep this verse in mind and continue in faith with a proper outlook toward trials, we can avoid merely <u>tolerating</u> and <u>putting up with</u> life and look forward to <u>thriving</u> and <u>prospering</u>.

ITEM NUMBER TWO – Not to downplay the hatred, resistance, and violence that Dr. Martin Luther King, Jr., and other leaders and participants in the Civil Rights Movement endured, but he had an interesting perspective about going to jail. While others might not be enamored with the thought of spending time incarcerated, Dr. King stated: "I catch up on my reading every time I go to jail."[22]

Is it possible to experience joy amidst trials? Not in the traditional way that people think of, with gladness and exuberance all around. However, I definitely believe that an inward, satisfying, sustaining joy is possible in the face of trials because nothing "is able to separate us from the love of God that is in Christ Jesus our Lord," which includes troubles, hardships, persecutions, famine, nakedness, danger, or sword (see Romans 8:35-39). Therefore, let us "catch up on our reading," i.e., let us seek the advantages of successfully managing trials discussed above. Let us seek the joy that we may have overlooked.

---

22. Malcolm Gladwell, *David and Goliath: Underdogs, Misfits, and the Art of Battling Giants* (New York: Back Bay Books, 2013), 188.

THE JOY AMIDST DEATH

"He is not here; he has risen, just as he said. Come and see the place where he lay . . . So the women hurried away from the tomb, afraid yet filled with joy, and ran to tell his disciples."

Matthew 28:6, 8

In one of her "alphabet mysteries," Sue Grafton's main character, Kinsey Millhone, is investigating an eighteen-year-old, unsolved murder of a high school girl. Millhone returns to the hometown and high school of the victim. Approaching the school, which is directly across from the town cemetery, she reflects in this manner:

> Just beyond the cemetery entrance and across the street, I saw the Lockaby Alternative High School. I wondered if the students made the same melancholy association: from Youth to Death with only a stone's throw between. When you're of high school age, the days go on forever and death's little more than a rumor at the end of the road. Dolan [her partner on the case] and I knew death was just a heartbeat away.[23]

---

23. Sue Grafton, *Q is for Quarry* (New York: G. P. Putnam's Sons, 2002), 226.

Death is not something we are terribly comfortable talking about. If we take time to ponder it, we do not come away with a warm, fuzzy feeling. After all, as Grafton's character indicates, life passes quickly and is fragile. Death can come very suddenly and interrupt cherished plans and relationships. The "rumor" can quickly become reality. Likewise, it is no respecter of persons. While we hope it comes at the end of a long and full life, this is not the way it necessarily happens. No doubt, all of us know of situations where an infant, a child, a teenager, a young adult, or someone else that we consider relatively young left this world prematurely. As many have said, "the old must die and the young may die." Death just isn't a very pleasant or popular topic. It's about the last item you would bring up in polite dinner conversation or discuss at a party, if you care about ever being invited back.

Given our aversion to this topic, it seems that people take different approaches when the subject surfaces. They may avoid talking about death altogether (just ask your family to sit down with you to go over your will, insurance papers, final wishes, etc., and see how quickly they come up with alternative questionable plans – "I think I'll be comparing the three major brands of orange juice at that time"). They may simply delay any discussion until a later time (and keep on doing so), or they may deflect thinking about death by resorting to humor which, in essence, is another form of avoidance. The writer, actor, movie director and producer, Woody Allen, once said, "I'm not afraid to die; I just don't want to be there when it happens." He is also reported to have said, "I don't want to accomplish immortality through my work; I want to achieve it by not dying." Actually, a little levity can be helpful at times but, certainly, neither humor nor sweeping the matter under the carpet should be our primary approach to managing this extremely important subject, with its eternal implications.

Eventually, the unescapable matter of death and dying needs to be confronted head-on. The good news is that God's people do not need to avoid the subject of death or to try to joke away its inevitability and earthly finality. With Christ as part of the conversation, death can be discussed in a far different light, even to the point of allowing joy to be part of our response. The verses mentioned at the opening of this chapter illustrate very well the double-edged nature of death. The women hurried away from the empty tomb "afraid yet filled with joy." It was unusual and a little unsettling to have talked with an angel, not something a person does every day. However, a staggering realization was now forming in their minds after what they had seen and heard. *Jesus wasn't there!* In God's power, He had overcome death and was alive. Death was still real, but now things had changed – it was not so foreboding and overwhelming as it had once been. Now there was an answer to this dark menace, this "last enemy," and the answer was and is the conquering Jesus Christ!

In our human moments when we are relying solely on our own thoughts and strength, fear can still be associated with death, principally when we think of when or how we might pass from this life. What can we do to dispel this fear? The answer comes in 2 Timothy 2:8a, "Remember Jesus Christ, raised from the dead . . ." As we do so, the promises and power of the risen Christ come fully into focus, and the thought of our own future victory over death fills us with hope and joy. Now it is not death that dominates the landscape and looms so large before us. Instead, it is Christ who supersedes all.

In the matter of death, we have another oxymoron before us. As with trials in the last chapter, the words "death" and "joy" do not naturally come together in our minds. And, as with trials, our purpose is not to trivialize death and its potential impact on our lives. Death leaves pain and loss and uncertainty about the future when it strikes. This is not to say that a few positive thoughts or religious sounding words will enable us to go on without feeling its enormity. Christians experience grief along with others and should never be told that tears and emotions have no place when the flood waters of death swell around us.

In that wonderful passage where Paul talks about the return of the Lord who will come "with a loud command, with the voice of the archangel and with the trumpet call of God, and the dead in Christ will rise first" (1 Thess. 4:16), he begins by saying, "Brothers, we do not want you to be ignorant about those who fall asleep, or to grieve like the rest of men, who have no hope" (vs. 13). Notice that Paul does not prohibit or discourage Christians from grieving. Given our human nature and the deep sense of loss that accompanies death, that would be unrealistic. He does, however, make a distinction. Our experience of death and grief is much different since we do not grieve as those who have "no hope." This is the message that will keep surfacing in the thoughts that follow. For Christians, words such as dread, fear, foreboding, and apprehension that are typically associated with death are replaced with words such as hope, power, victory, and even joy.

The Scriptures say some very interesting and comforting things about death. Let's turn our attention to a few of these wonderful thoughts and phrases.

Death is a shadow. Obviously, our reference point here is Psalm 23:4 - "Even though I walk through the valley of the shadow of death, I will fear no evil, for you are with me: your rod and your staff, they comfort me." At times, the shepherd may take the sheep through dark valleys and ravines in the ongoing search for "green pastures" and "quiet waters." Wild beasts, robbers, and death could be lurking in these places, but the sheep are not aware that anything might be amiss and are not troubled because of the presence of the shepherd. In the same manner, just as the shepherd of the Old Testament was prepared to lead and protect his sheep through the darkest valleys, so the Good Shepherd of the New Testament goes with us through our darkest valleys, the darkest of all being death.

Years ago, I remember a piece by C. S. Lovett. He was discussing the time that Jesus raised Lazarus from the dead in John 11. As you may recall, Lazarus had already been in the grave for four days when Jesus arrived, a sure sign (supposedly) that there was nothing that even He could do. Jesus, however, miraculously raised him from the dead and restored him to life in this world. In a very memorable phrase, Lovett concluded that Lazarus was "unimpressed with death." In Christ, we, too, can be "unimpressed with death" for now it is just a shadow that we pass through when we go to be with the Lord.

Death is precious. This unexpected, extraordinary thought about death comes from Psalm 116:15 - "Precious in the sight of the LORD is the death of his saints." A couple of ideas are associated with the word "precious." When we talk about gold as a "precious metal," we mean it is very valuable and desirable. So, to God, our lives are extremely valuable and dying is a precious moment when the valuable and costly commodity of a faithful servant's life departs this earthly world.

The term "precious" also refers to something that is "beloved" and "dear." Thus, children and grandchildren, hugs and kisses, puppies and kittens, and memories of special times are some of the things that we refer to as "precious." Under normal circumstances, we would never think of placing death in the same category with the other items just mentioned, as something very dear. However, by dying on the cross and rising again after three days, Christ has turned the world of death upside down. Now, when we pass into the eternal glory of the Lord, it can be viewed as something precious, as we exchange the cares of this life for our heavenly home with Him. D. Martyn Lloyd-Jones led London's Westminster Chapel as pastor and preacher for thirty-two years, beginning in 1943. He was one of Britain's greatest Bible expositors and the author of many books that are still read today. Just before his death at the age of 81, he reportedly told his family, "Don't pray for healing, don't hold me back from the glory." Lloyd-Jones could express such an attitude because he knew that the death of the faithful is precious and dear in God's sight and the gateway to an even fuller and more remarkable life in His presence.

Death is disarmed. In our age, we know about disarmament. We seek to disarm and remove the things that are dangerous and deadly, that have the power to destroy. Consequently, we talk about disarming bombs, nuclear weapons, and individuals wielding guns and knives. Paul speaks about death in similar language – "'Death has been swallowed up in victory.' 'Where, O death is your victory? Where, O death is your sting?' The sting of death is sin, and the power of sin is the law. But thanks be to God! He gives us the victory through our Lord Jesus Christ" (1 Cor. 15:54b-57).

Did you notice that Paul seems to be taunting death in these words. Actually, his tone is rather amusing. In essence, he is saying, "What happened to your swagger, death? You used to intimidate us, harass us, and laugh in our faces, but now you are no longer yourself. Ha! You have been disarmed. Your sting and your bite are gone, like a wasp with no stinger or a snake with no venom. The stage is no longer yours, with you as the star player. What do you think of that?"

It reminds me of the *Rocky III* movie when Rocky Balboa says to his nemesis Clubber Lang who has knocked him senseless in a previous boxing match, "You ain't so bad! Come on, you ain't so bad! You ain't nothing!" This is exactly the message that Paul is conveying as regards death. It no longer is "so bad." It no longer is the dreaded, demoralizing, and terrifying force that it once was. It still touches us since sin has brought it into the world, and we have to pass through it as we exit this life. However, death no longer commands us and dominates us. Christ commands and dominates in the moment of death, for He has disarmed its power and strength.

Death is abolished. Not only is death disarmed, it is also abolished. Paul speaks of Christ as the One "*who* has abolished death and brought life and immortality to light through the gospel" (2 Timothy 1:10b, NKJV). The meaning is that the power and effects of death are no longer active in our lives. In Sicily, Mt. Etna was about fifty miles from our house and very visible as it towered in the distance. It is an active volcano and, on several occasions, we could see red hot streams of lava flowing down its slopes at night after it had erupted. If Mt. Etna suddenly became inactive and no longer posed a threat to nearby towns and residents, it would provide us with the same picture that we have here of death – previous activity replaced with inactivity (spiritually speaking); previous danger replaced with no longer needing to fret and worry.

The book of Hebrews also speaks about this matter: "Since the children have flesh and blood, he too shared in their humanity so that by his death he might destroy him who holds the power of death – that is, the devil – and free those who all their lives were held in slavery by their fear of death" (2:14-15). The message is that Christ took up residency with us, adding our human nature to His divine nature, so that He could ultimately demonstrate power superior to that of the devil and death by going to the Cross and experiencing death but not succumbing to it. With His victory, we are freed from any slavery to the fear of death.

Christ, then, has abolished and destroyed death and, according to our verse in 2 Tim. 1:10, has also "brought life and immortality to light through the gospel." Christ holds up what life can truly be and reveals that, in Him, it leads to immortality. Life is not intended to be looked upon as merely moving in the direction of death. In the picture that Christ unveils, death is no longer held up as the ultimate end, the destination of all things. True life here, surrounded by the strength and friendship of God and Christ and the Holy Spirit, followed by immortality is the goal and destination for the faithful – this is the ultimate end. The gospel of Christ brings all of this to light. Instead of death, we now look forward to that heavenly home where there is no death (Rev. 21:4) or night (Rev. 22:5), only the glory of God and the light of the lamb (Rev. 21:23).

Death is gain. Again, we turn to the apostle Paul: "For to me, to live is Christ and to die is gain" (Philippians 1:21). For Paul, meaningful living is all about knowing and serving Christ. It is not about being wrapped up in some of the typical pursuits that many substitute for true living, e.g., acquiring, getting ahead, recognition, worldly gratification, or becoming a power broker. It is about loving and being loved by the great Lord of the universe; consequently, remaining in this life means more opportunities to further His purposes while dying means to experience the fullness of His eternal presence. This is another word that we do not normally associate with death. Words that usually come to mind are "loss," "separation," "ruin," and "devastation." Paul, to the contrary, calls it "gain."

Before, we noticed that Paul seemed to be taunting death. Here, he appears to be very casual and indifferent, lacking in any major concern about death and refusing to be bothered by its bloated reputation. His tone in this passage is rather nonchalant as he goes back and forth discussing the merits of whether it is best to continue in this life, which he concludes is best for the Philippians, or to depart and be with Christ which, for him, would be far better. From his overall attitude, we do not sense that he is discussing one of the hot topics that weighs heavily on the minds of men and women. Paul is so at ease with the subject of death that he might be talking about almost any point of conversation, e.g., whether to go to Corinth or to Ephesus. He doesn't get all worked up about the "nasty" nature of death. The only thing he gets worked up and excited about is the prospect of being with Christ!

When Paul talks about his desire "to depart and be with Christ" in verse twenty-three, one of the images of the word "depart" is that of a ship casting off its mooring lines and setting sail. I am reminded of these beautiful words, entitled "The Ship":

I am standing upon the seashore. A ship at my side spreads her white sails to the morning breeze and starts for the blue ocean. She is an object of beauty and strength, and I stand and watch her until at length she is only a ribbon of white cloud just where the sea and sky come to mingle with each other. Then someone at my side says, "There! She's gone!"

Gone where? Gone from my sight – that is all. She is just as large in mast and hull and spar as she was when she left my side, and just as able to bear her load of living freight – to the place of destination. Her diminished size is in me, not in her, and just at the moment when someone at my side says, "There! She's gone!" there are other voices ready to take up the glad shout, "There! She comes!" and that is dying.[24]

The bottom line is that *death is destroyed*; now, we merely journey through death to our heavenly destination where we "will receive a rich welcome into the eternal kingdom of our Lord and Savior Jesus Christ" (2 Peter 1:11).

When our son got married several years ago, not only did Amie become a part of our family, but her children – Bobby, Mykala, and Levi – did so as well. Before the wedding, they all came to visit so we could get acquainted. The children, ages four through seven at the time, had not had much contact with the military prior to knowing me. The War on Terrorism was about two months old when they came and, somehow, it came up in the conversation around the dinner table. Bobby asked, "Did anyone die in the war today?" I answered that I didn't know of anyone who had died that day. Then, Mykala wanted to know, "Could you get killed?" Being a noncombatant, I replied that I didn't think that I would, but it could happen. She went on to ask, "What will happen to you if you die?" My answer was that I trusted that I

24. W. E. Sangster, *Can I Know God? and Other Sermons* (New York: Abingdon Press, 1960), 176.

would go to heaven. Levi, the youngest, thought for a few seconds and then piped in, "Yes, if you die, Jesus will fix you up and make you alive again."

Joy may not be the first thought that comes to mind or the first emotion that we experience when death touches our lives. We need to manage the human side of grief of no longer having loved ones with us, or the prospect of our own passage from this life. Still, there can, indeed, be an underlying sense of confidence and even joy for us and for those we cherish when we focus on the reality that Jesus will fix us up and make us alive again and that we will be in His presence forever. This happens because, in God and Christ, death is a shadow, it is precious, it is disarmed, it is abolished, it is gain, and it is destroyed.

THE JOY OF GOD'S WORD

"I rejoice in following your statutes as one rejoices in great
riches. I meditate on your precepts and consider your ways. I
delight in your decrees; I will not neglect your word."

Psalm 119:14-16

Judy and I went to a book signing a few years ago. The writer was David
Baldacci, author of a number of best-selling mystery-thrillers. Before starting
the signing session, Baldacci spoke for about twenty minutes and told several
interesting anecdotes. One of the items he mentioned was about having his
books published in Italy. After success here in the States, his books began to
be published in other countries. Just before going to press in Italy for the first
time, Baldacci's Italian publisher called and indicated that he wanted to come
up with a different name, a pseudonym. According to the publisher, Italians
didn't believe that one of their own could write good mystery-thrillers and,
for his books to sell well in Italy, Baldacci needed a good American name.

The publisher pressed for a quick response. As Baldacci was thinking,
he looked out the window and saw his vehicle; consequently, he said, "How
about David Ford?" The publisher thought that was a great name to go by

and, therefore, Baldacci's first books printed in Italian listed the author as David Ford. Later on, Baldacci became David B. Ford and, finally, after much success in the Italian market, his books were printed and distributed using his real name. It turns out that a person of Italian heritage can write exciting mystery-thrillers.

It also turns out that fishermen, shepherds, tax collectors, and prophets can write good literature and have left us the best-selling and most beloved book of all time, the Bible. However, this book (this collection of books) is unlike any other and has a distinction that sets it apart from other writings – it is divinely inspired and shares with us the very thoughts and mind of God. While this reality can be somewhat intimidating at times, it also is the source of tremendous joy. Other works of literature can attempt to tell us about God, share opinions, or speculate about God, but the Bible gives us direct access to what God thinks and to what He thinks we need to know. How exciting is that!

As was just mentioned, the Holy Scriptures can be a little intimidating and may not always bring joy into our lives initially. God is not interested in having us develop into "fair weather Christians" or "Sunday morning Christians" or quasi-Christians, picking and choosing what we will observe based on what is convenient or popular or on what *we* think is fitting and necessary in the twenty-first century. His Word has lots of things to say, for instance, about honesty, priorities, the treatment of others, the use and place of money, and sexual practices. Thus, the initial impact the Bible has on us may be one of bringing us under conviction or even one of avoidance, since our own practices may be at variance with what the Scriptures are saying. If we have a decent conscience, it is never fun to be at odds with what the Word of God has to say. But, in the long run, when we arrive at seeking to do His will and walk in His ways, this collection of writings that is both ancient and in tune with human nature and the needs of society today leads to joy and gladness. It turns out that these are the words that we need, above all others, for fulfillment and direction in this life and for preparation for the life to come.

I think there are at least four reasons why joy and the Word of God go hand-in-hand. Let's search them out.

The Word of God comes to us from without. What we basically have in mind with this statement is that the Bible is not just another voice from within the human family. All other writings, statements, arguments, and opinions about God, how life should be lived, what life is all about, what is important, and where all of this is headed come from the minds of men and women. This being the case, all these thoughts are based on speculation or feelings, or they are guesses, sometimes educated and sometimes not so educated. As a result, these thoughts and opinions from within may be helpful (when they complement and coincide with what God has said) or they can be downright bizarre and greatly misguided. Who wants to throw in with the idea that money and possessions are the only things worth pursuing or that the only person who really matters is "me"? Well, apparently many do throw in with such thinking, but I would contend that this is not the road that leads to a satisfying way of life either for us as individuals or as a society. The road of life is littered with disillusioned souls who bought in to such temporary and superficial values.

Of course, for skeptics, the comeback is that the Bible was recorded by men and, therefore, is in the same boat with everything else that has ever been penned. This is where people of faith part ways with such humanistic thinking. We don't understand all that inspiration means and all of the process by which the books of the Bible came into being, but we definitely believe that the Scriptures were written in a way that differs from how other books in human history were composed. Yes, men were involved but far more was taking place.

There are several key verses/passages that speak to these matters. Two of them are found in the first chapter of 2 Peter:

> We did not follow cleverly invented stories when we told you about the power and coming of our Lord Jesus Christ, but we were eyewitnesses of his majesty. For he received honor and glory from God the Father when the voice came to him from the Majestic Glory, saying, "This is my Son, whom I love; with him I am well pleased." We ourselves heard this voice that came from heaven when we were with him on the sacred mountain (2 Peter 1:16-18).

Among other things, these verses speak to the fact that Peter was an eyewitness to the events that he talks about. Consequently, we have confidence in what he shares with us. Here, he specifically introduces the subject of Christ's return. While some discount this possibility, Peter states that he has already witnessed a preview, if you please, of this glorious future occasion. He, along with James and John, were with Jesus on the Mount of Transfiguration when the glory of Christ was revealed and "the voice came to him from the Majestic Glory, saying, 'This is my Son, whom I love; with him I am well pleased.'" Peter had previously observed Christ's "honor and glory" firsthand; thus, the return of Christ in great glory is hardly out of the question or open to debate. Peter knows that our Lord possesses glory and power beyond all others.

Not all accounts regarding our Lord are based on personal observation and personally being present for the events of His life. Luke tells us that the Gospel that he wrote came about after "carefully investigating everything from the beginning" concerning the life of Christ (see Luke 1:1-4). Still, his investigation relied on "eyewitnesses and servants of the word." The Gospel and Epistles that John and Peter left for posterity, however, required no research because they were there for all that happened during the ministry of Jesus. No playing fast and loose with the facts, no making things up or going on hearsay, no integrity issues to raise our eyebrows over, just folks who had been there and are as creditable as you can get.

When I was growing up in Ohio, Waite Hoyt was the radio voice of the Cincinnati Reds baseball team. Hoyt had been an accomplished major league player in his own right, having pitched for the New York Yankees during much of the Babe Ruth era. In fact, Hoyt won twenty-two games for the 1927 team that is regarded as one of the best teams of all time. He was a teammate of Babe Ruth for nearly ten years.

As we know, many stories and legends about Babe Ruth have arisen over the years, some of them perhaps hard to believe but still accurate as Ruth did more than most who have ever played the game. On the other hand, some of the stories have, no doubt, been embellished seeking to add to Ruth's heroic and iconic status. I remember Hoyt reminiscing from time to time about the Babe's exploits and antics. His stories could be trusted because he was there, an eyewitness to the events he was talking about. He wasn't sharing things that he had heard from someone else, who had heard it from someone else and just might have altered it in passing it along. He had lived it, was a trustworthy and honorable person, and could be counted on to know what he was talking about.

In the same way, the things that Peter and John and Matthew tell us about Jesus are not "cleverly invented stories" but come from trustworthy individuals who lived these events and are providing us with the most reliable accounts possible. Besides this, there is something else to consider about the words that come to us in Scripture. Peter describes this as he continues in verses 19-21:

> And we have the word of the prophets made more
> certain, and you will do well to pay attention to it, as to

a light shining in a dark place, until the day dawns and the morning star rises in your hearts. Above all, you must understand that no prophecy of Scripture came about by the prophet's own interpretation. For prophecy never had its origin in the will of man, but men spoke from God as they were carried along by the Holy Spirit.

As some might doubt what Peter is saying about the coming day of glory for Christ, so they might also doubt what the prophets have said at various times about "the day of the Lord" when all things will culminate in God's victory over evil and salvation for His people. In this matter, too, we do not have to fret about the reliability of what the prophets and the Scriptures tell us because their thoughts were guided by the Holy Spirit. It is true that these thoughts were put down in writing by men, but the thoughts are not just what they came up with on their own. "Let's see, wouldn't it be nice if the day would come when God's Messiah will overcome all the nonsense, injustice, and evil in the world; when all things will be put right and the people of God will triumph and live in His presence. I think I'll write about that to give folks some hope and encouragement, even if I'm not 100% sure that things will really play out that way."

Instead of such an approach, the prophets were "inspired" and "carried along" by God's Spirit so that what comes to us is truly from God with the full assurance and approval of His divine involvement. Again, we do not understand all the mechanics of the inspiration process. Since the biblical writers demonstrate their own vocabulary, style, and phraseology, it wasn't that they just sat down and daydreamed or dozed off while the Holy Spirit moved their pens. Their individually comes through in what was written down. However, we also know that the end result is what God wanted us to know and what He sanctions. Holy Scripture is not what men willed, what they came up with, or merely what they thought was important. Men were the instruments for relaying the very message, ideas, and work of God.

Other passages weigh in on this theme as well. Listen to what Douglas Moo has to say on the subject of "inspiration":

> "Inspiration" means "breathed in"; and Christian theologians use this word to describe the quality of Scripture according to which it is the product of God's "breathing" his words into it. Perhaps the classic text is 2 Timothy 3:16: "All Scripture is God-breathed and is useful for teaching, rebuking, correcting, and training in righteousness." "Scripture" here is, of course, the Old Testament; but the text establishes that whatever appropriately be considered "Scripture" carries the quality of being "God-breathed." Jesus attests to the same idea, when, in response to Satan's temptation, he cites Deuteronomy 8:3: "'Man does not live on bread alone, but on every word that comes from the mouth of God'" (Matt. 4:4). Likewise, the author of Hebrews begins his letter by noting that "in the past God spoke to our forefathers through the prophets," and he repeatedly attributes the words of the Old Testament to God (e.g., 4:7; 8:8) and the Holy Spirit (e.g., 3:7; 10:15).[25]

Paul adds some more to the discussion about the divine origin of Scripture when he says: "I want you to know, brothers, that the gospel I preached is not something that man made up. I did not receive it from any man, nor was I taught it; rather, I received it by revelation from Jesus Christ" (Gal. 1:11-12). All of these verses, and others, point to the marvelous reality that, while conveyed through men, the Word of God comes from without. It

---

25. Douglas J. Moo, *2 Peter and Jude: the NIV Application Commentary, from Biblical Text . . . to Contemporary Life*, the NIV Application Commentary Series, vol. 18, ed. Terry Muck, et al. (Grand Rapids, MI: Zondervan Publishing House, 1996), 84.

comes from beyond the mere experiences, minds, and conclusions of men, and, consequently, is unique and authoritative in a way that exceeds all other writings. Some of the books come from those who were eyewitnesses to what they passed along. All of them come from men who were guided by the Holy Spirit of God.

Another reason why joy and the Bible are linked together is because *the Word of God communicates and reveals God to us.* We have already touched upon this in our opening discussion, but we need to realize how privileged we are not only to have this Word from without but to have clear communication about who God is and what He desires from and for us. The fact that the Scriptures communicate God and His ways to us enables us to live in victorious fellowship with Him. For this, we truly rejoice.

The importance of communication can be seen in an embarrassing phone conversation I had during my last tour as a chaplain. I was in the office one morning and a Religious Program Specialist called to talk. He began the conversation, I thought, by saying, "I'm calling from my rack." You may know that a "rack" is what the military refers to as one's bunk or bed. I thought it was a little unusual that he wanted me to know he was calling from his sleeping quarters, but I let it pass and just proceeded to chat.

This individual and I had served together at a previous duty station. His present tour was about to end, and he was calling to inquire about the vacancy in our office that would open up about the time he was ready to move. He wanted to know what it was like to work with submariners, about the housing situation, what the area had to offer, etc. So, we caught up on old times for a few minutes, I answered his questions, and we said a cordial "goodbye."

After hanging up, it still puzzled me that he had opened by talking about his rack. I thought about it for several minutes, and then the light bulb finally came on. He wasn't calling from his rack, he was calling from Iraq! All the time we were talking, I never once showed any concern for his situation, never once asked if he was safe and how he was getting along in a combat zone. I just merrily carried as if it was no big deal that he was in Iraq risking his life every day. I felt terrible when I finally processed it all. I wanted to call right back and let him know that I wasn't the insensitive, cold-hearted jerk that he had every right to conclude that I was, but I didn't have his phone number to do so. Fortunately, he called back several weeks later upon his return to the States, and I was able to explain what had happened and beg for his forgiveness. He took it well and seemed to understand, letting me off the hook. It ended in a good place, but I was certainly stirred up for a while because I missed the communication and did not understand what exactly was going on.

Without the Word of God, we would not have a clear communication about God. We would have to carry on, filling in the blanks as best as we could. And, since there would be no lack of voices spouting their opinions, we would just have to choose what we think is the best of the alternatives out there and hope that it was right. Thanks be to God that this is not our situation! We are not left to flounder on the seas of "maybe this, maybe that" because the Word brings God and His message into sharp focus. Granted, there may be parts of the Scriptures that we do not fully understand (e.g., exactly what Jesus did when "He went and preached to the spirits in prison" in 1 Peter 3:18-20), but the Bible provides all we need to know about God so that we can have a viable relationship with God the Father, God the Son, and God the Holy Spirit.

So, just what do we know about God from the communication that the Word provides? Obviously, there are too many things to mention them all here, but some of the basics are that God is omnipotent, omnipresent, and omniscient. "Omnipotent" means that God is all-powerful. "Scripture often affirms that all power belongs to God (Ps.147:5), that all things are possible for God (Luke 1:37; Matt. 19:26), and that God's power exceeds what humans can ask or think (Eph. 3:20)."[26] "Omnipresent" means that God is present everywhere at once. Psalm 139:7-12 informs us that there is no place we can go and elude the presence of God. And, "omniscient" means that God is all-knowing. Speaking of omniscient, did you hear about the middle-aged man who was taken to the hospital with a heart attack. While he is on the operating table, he has a near death experience and sees God. He asks God if this is it. God says "no" and explains that he has another 30 years to live.

After recovering and with a new lease on life, the man decides to stay in the hospital a little longer and have a face lift, liposuction, bicep augmentation, and a tummy tuck. He even has someone come in and change his hair color. When all is done, he walks out of the hospital and is run over by an ambulance speeding to the hospital. He arrives before God and complains, "I thought you said I had another 30 years to live." God replies, "I'm sorry, but I didn't recognize you!" We can be assured that this will never happen because God knows all and will never be confused as to who we are. Likewise, He is all-powerful and present everywhere.

These are tremendous attributes of God with no one else among us even scratching the surface of such power, knowledge, and all-reaching presence. However, they are not terribly personal characteristics when it comes to relating to God and fellowshipping with Him. Thankfully, the Scriptures also reveal that God is a personal Being who loves us and desires to interact with us. I have always been encouraged by what Jesus said in John 14:23: "If anyone loves me, he will obey my teaching. My Father will love him, and we will come to him and make our home with him."

What a marvelous promise! When we love God and seek His will, God and Christ come to us. Notice that this is not merely a quick check-up visit.

---

26. Brand and Mitchell, *Holman Illustrated Bible Dictionary*, 1191.

With God being so busy, we might think that He would stop by, ask us how we're doing, remind us of His love, and then be on His way – "I'm sorry this has to be so short, but I've got lots of other people and things to attend to. I'm sure you understand – running the universe isn't easy." Even this would be nice, and we would understand if God had to hurry on His way. But the promise involves more than a hasty health and welfare check. Jesus states that they plan to stop and linger and take up residence with us. They plan to move in which is accomplished through the presence of the Holy Spirit. This concept is mind-boggling, but the reality is that God promises to live with us in order to encourage, empower, reassure, and guide us. You can't get any more personal than that!

So, in addition to being omnipotent, omnipresent, and omniscient and other attributes such as being the creator, sustainer, and ruler of all things, God is also a loving and personal God who doesn't just stop by periodically but who actually "sets up house" in our lives. That favorite verse of so many, John 3:16, reminds us of the depth of God's love: "For God so loved the world that he gave his one and only Son, that whoever believes in him shall not perish but have eternal life." God loves us so much that He spared nothing in order to deal with our sin and separation from Him, allowing Christ to leave His heavenly home and come here to die on the Cross, the sinless for the sinful. Then, this loving God always lives with us and in us, as we already learned in these verses about the Holy Spirit – "And I will ask the Father, and he will give you another Counselor to be with you forever – the Spirit of truth. The world cannot accept him, because it neither sees him nor knows him. But you know him, for he lives with you and will be in you" (John 14:16-17).

Let us rejoice that the Bible has been given to us and preserved down through the ages, for it communicates and reveals God to us. The wonderful advantage this provides is that we don't have to guess about the all-powerful and loving nature of God.

A couple of other items also contribute to the connection between joy and the Word of God. One of them is this: *"Your word is a lamp to my feet and a light for my path"* (Psalm 119:105).

We live in a world of great beauty and variety, created and given to us by God. Most people that we encounter are generous and gracious, trying to do good things. Unfortunately, there are others who become misguided and get off track, who get caught up in power and money and the "me" syndrome, living as if things revolve around their desires and that they can do whatever they please. Consequently, we also encounter a fair amount of crud in the world. Like me, perhaps you have noticed such things as the following:

— vulgar words and rude behavior are commonplace in the public arena.

— several, not all, "stars" (supposedly role models) of music, motion pictures, sports, etc., do drugs, get drunk, and frequent questionable places.

— people say bad things about others and call them every awful name they can think of simply because they have a different opinion on political and other issues.

— the pornography business is very profitable and stories of sexual predators regularly appear in the daily news.

— many companies cannot sell their products without utilizing some kind of sexual appeal, even though they may be selling tires for your car or jogging shoes for your feet.

— TV and motion pictures do not shy away from violence and every conceivable sexual activity, whether the activity is healthy and edifying or not. Even the music we buy has a rating system so we can determine if it is fit for human consumption.

— And, of course, wars continue to be fought around the world.

We need light and guidance. We need to know what is good and beneficial. We need to know how best to conduct ourselves so that we can get along with one another, avoid pitfalls that cause havoc and pain, and promote those things that lead to the best way of life possible. The light we need comes from the Word of God.

Without light, things get dangerous. Try walking around in an unfamiliar house in the dark – your toes and shins may never be the same. Try jogging down a dark street – unexpected potholes won't be kind to your legs and ankles, maybe your head if you trip and fall down. Growing up, the kids in our neighborhood played baseball nearly every day in the summer. Sometimes, we played into twilight and beyond since it was our passion and maybe one team needed their last at bat. It wasn't always the smartest thing to do – who wants to get smacked by a line drive that you can't see coming?

Indeed, we need light so that we don't misstep and end up stumbling and hurting ourselves. This is definitely true in our spiritual lives just as it is in our physical lives, and the Scriptures are the only universally proven source of light that we can trust for illuminating our paths at all times. Too much crud swirls around us for us to sort it all out on our own. We can learn some things by trial and error, but who knows what condition our lives and relationships will be in before we finally get it right. A wonderful phrase occurs in Deuteronomy 6:24. The people of God are encouraged to honor the Lord and observe His decrees because to do so is "for our good always" (NKJV). The Word of God isn't trying to crimp our style or deny us experiences that others may be indulging in and promoting; it is simply striving to provide light so that we enjoy the best way of life possible and avoid the dangers that lurk in places where we don't need to go.

Finally, joy and the Word of God go hand in hand because *it is the great means of living an overcoming life*. Again, this thought has similarities with what we have just considered, but we can't leave this discussion without mentioning Psalm 119:11 – "I have hidden your word in my heart that I might not sin against you." Having portions of Scripture, the thoughts of God, tucked away in our hearts and minds empowers us in moments of temptation when we are in danger of straying from where we belong.

Another characteristic of God that we didn't mention before is that He is a God of holiness, righteousness, and morality. And, yes, there are places where we do not belong and temptations to overcome, not because God is trying to strike "fun" from our lives but because those places and temptations take us away from holiness and righteousness and are devastating to the good life that God has in mind for us.

During my years as a Navy chaplain, I gave talks on "human values" or included this theme in the presentations I gave to newly reporting sailors. The Navy holds up Honor, Courage, and Commitment as its front-line values, so I talked about these and others that enrich our lives and help us get to where we want to be, e.g., honesty, responsibility, respect for others, an honest days' work for an honest days' pay, etc. Certainly, spiritual values came into play as well. I frequently used a motion picture as an illustration to drive home one of my points. The movie is an older one, but it still serves our purposes here.

I began by telling about watching the film *Same Time Next Year* in the wardroom onboard ship. An evening movie is, generally, shown onboard Navy ships for those who are off duty, unless some kind of evolution is taking place. The movie stars Alan Alda (of *M*A*S*H* television fame and numerous other acting roles) and the actress, Ellen Burstyn. It is a comedy and I decided to stay since Alda was quite humorous in his role as "Hawkeye" Pierce on *M*A*S*H*. The movie turns out to be very funny and those of us watching it had a lot of good laughs. But, as the film rolls along, it dawns on me that what we're all laughing about is adultery. The story line is that two people, on vacation from their families and work, meet annually at a seaside lodge in New England and, eventually, "link up." The movie chronicles their rendezvous' over the years and what is taking place in their lives each new time they meet. Some of it is poignant, but it is mainly a comedy designed for laughs and a good time. The only redeeming factor (if it can be called "redeeming") is that they finally decide to stay with their spouses and families.

After giving this background for the sailor, I would make this point – adultery looks very different in my office than it does on the silver screen (or TV or literature or wherever else it surfaces in a light-hearted, casual way). Unfortunately, I have dealt with this subject time and time again in my counseling, and it is never humorous, rewarding, or appealing when it is forced upon couples. Even if undetected, it is a world of lies and deception that interrupts the flow, growth, and happiness of the marriage and family. The result – folks end up in a place where God never intended them to be, with significant heartache and pain.

This is what we are often up against as we attempt to live life in a godly fashion. The "world" takes things that are not good and healthy, presents them as harmless and innocent, makes us laugh and smile at them, encourages us to think that it doesn't really matter all that much or that it's prudish and judgmental to not go along, and bombards us with "the message of the day" over and over again. After hearing the propaganda so many times, seeing "beautiful people" supposedly enjoying it, and laughing at it because of the way that it is packaged and presented, our concern takes a nose dive and our moral alarm system no longer goes off. And, guess what? We then jump in ourselves, but we reap consequences and hardships that the filmmakers, writers, and others conveniently left out.

What can be done? Several things, such as to be alert and to flee from compromising situations before they fully develop, but, primarily, to pray, to surround ourselves with godly influences, and to hide God's Word in our hearts. This latter item allows the Holy Spirit to bring God's ways and thoughts quickly to mind and steer us away from whatever enticing allurement is knocking at the door. Having a plan and the power to avoid the menacing, crippling intrusion of sin brings incomprehensible joy into our lives.

The Word of God and joy are inseparably linked because the Scriptures are a Word from without, they communicate and reveal God to us, they are a lamp and a light to guide us through life, and they are the means to living an overcoming life. True, it is not the hilarious or the general type of joy that the world constantly pursues but the ultimate, abiding, fullness of joy that comes from having a map that enables us to successfully navigate through this world and enjoy sweet communion with our Lord. We do well to remember the old saying, "A Bible that is falling apart usually belongs to someone who isn't."

THE JOY OF CHRISTIAN LIVING

"Serve the LORD with gladness;
come before him with joyful songs."

Psalm 100:2

Not very long ago, another technology wonder toy hit the market with all kinds of fanfare and hoopla. There were long lines at certain stores to be one of the first to own one of these "must have," latest technology items that anyone who considers themselves on the cutting edge couldn't be without. An insightful editorial cartoon by John Darkow appeared in the *Columbia* (Mo.) *Daily Tribune* at the time. Two friends were shown trying to figure out their new modern marvel. The first one says, "It's got a cell phone, video iPod, e-mail terminal, web browser, camera, alarm clock, palm-type organizer . . . ". Looking confused, the second one says, "Which icon do I touch to 'get a life'?"

This is the pressing question for all of us as humans – how do I get a life? What is the best course to pursue for living life to the fullest? Do gadgets and gizmos provide the best opportunities for excitement and fulfillment? Do possessions and getting ahead of everyone else lead to satisfaction and a sense that I am on the fast track to a worthwhile existence? There are many around us who proclaim such philosophies with great fervor and passion. However, the Scriptures indicate differently. When we turn to the wisdom of God's Word, the best approach to experience true joy in life is to live a godly life and now, since the coming of Christ, a Christian life. Other approaches only result in momentary, shallow encounters with joy and life. Other approaches only weave in and out of "general" joy but do not land us in the midst of "ultimate" joy.

Recently, I saw a man with a T-shirt expressing his view on this subject. The message on the shirt declared, "Life Begins . . . When You Get One." Interposed between the top and bottom lines of this thought was the emblem of a very famous motorcycle company (the one with the very distinct rumbling sound). I'm not here to criticize motorcycles (a lot of people seem to enjoy them), but I would challenge the notion that you don't have a life unless you have one, or that life is suddenly transformed to an elevated and meaningful existence when you drive one off the dealer's lot. I don't know from personal experience, but perhaps there is something to be said about the freedom of driving down the road with the wind blowing in your face on a beautiful, clear day. There may be something to be said, too, about sitting drenched under a highway overpass waiting for the downpour to pass.

The point is that the "things" of life may provide us with some enjoyment and entertainment, perhaps some security, but the reality is that life begins, continues at its best, and ends in the best possible scenario with God, Christ, and the Holy Spirit. This may seem like a bold statement when the opinion of the godly/Christian life sometimes is that it is too rigid and confining. Certainly, there are guidelines and standards to keep in mind when God's people interact with the "world"; however, I believe, as Christians, that we can still go to concerts and movies (within reason). I believe we can still go to theme parks, ride motorcycles, listen to music, go boating, play golf, etc., as long as these activities do not crowd out/interfere with our number one priority of honoring God in our lives. The items we are encouraged to be alert to and avoid are only the things that are not going to enrich us, build us up, and get us to where we want to be in our lives and relationships.

So, why is there wonderful joy in the Christian life and why is it the best way of life going?

What does it offer that commends itself to us and others? We have already considered several answers to these very questions. The Christian life offers the joy of God's presence, power, and friendship for our daily lives. There is joy in the salvation and forgiveness that comes through Christ. Joy comes from worshipping and uplifting God. It comes from being able to communicate with God through prayer at any time, for any situation. There is joy in the reality that death has been conquered. We have looked at these and other reasons why the Christian life is so joyful and beneficial. Now, let us add a few more reasons to the extensive list as to why the Christian life can be regarded as the best life to pursue.

In the Christian life, we are supported by a firm foundation. As we noted in Chapter One, being centered in Christ means that our lives are anchored on the rock of His wisdom and knowledge, not on the sands of what is currently being trumpeted as desirable and in vogue. Furthermore, the New Testament tells us that abundant life comes through Christ (John 10:10), that we "have been given fullness in Christ" (Colossians 2:8-10), and that we "take hold of the life that is truly life" by putting our hope in God (1 Timothy 6:1-19). In Christ, as the verses in Colossians state, we are not taken captive "through hollow and deceptive philosophy, which depends on human traditions and the basic principles of this world rather than on Christ." Indeed, in Christ we are grounded in the richness and fullness of His ways and all-encompassing power.

Our Lord weighed in on these matters with "The Parable of the Rich

Fool" in Luke 12:13-21.

If we think possessions and worldly gain should be the pursuits of choice, think again. This parable, as you may recall, is about the rich man whose fields produced bountifully, so much so that he had to tear down his old barns and build new and bigger ones to accommodate the harvest. The problem wasn't that he was materially blessed with plenty to live on, but that God was nowhere in his thoughts and plans, and there was no thought of sharing his good fortune with anyone else. "And I'll say to myself, 'You have plenty of good things laid up for many years. Take life easy; eat, drink, and be merry" (verse 19). Jesus, however, knowing that all of this was fleeting and could be gone in an instant (see verse 20), proclaimed: "Watch out! Be on your guard against all kinds of greed; a man's life does not consist in the abundance of his possessions" (verse 15). The secret to a meaningful life, He concluded, does not lie with "the abundance of possessions" but with the abundance of God, i.e., to be "rich toward God" (verse 21). For me, this is one of the great thoughts and phrases of the Bible, that we should seek to be "rich toward God."

I have a devotional that I have given over the years that I think ties in at this point. It is entitled, "Advice for Life," and the thoughts speak to centering our lives on the foundation of Christ and not just wandering aimlessly about, hoping that some half-baked idea from the world may, eventually, turn out to be half-way decent. Here are four thoughts that I believe will keep us tracking toward true joy and true life, and being "rich toward God":

Let us seek to deepen our lives, not merely expand our lives. As we interact with others, we often like to say that we have been to a major sporting event ("It wasn't easy getting those tickets to the World Series, or the Super Bowl, or the Indy 500"). We like to say that we have traveled ("I don't think I could have eaten another bite on that Caribbean cruise"). We like to indicate that we know our way around gourmet food ("Don't you just love sushi?", or "The French cuisine we had last week was ever so tasty"). We like to promote a cultured image ("The symphony, or the opera, or the touring Broadway play was just grand the other night"). Certainly, there is nothing wrong per se with any of these items; I like eating out, traveling, and going to special events just as much as the next person. However, to be prepared for life and all the options it throws before us requires that we not merely expand our lives but that we also deepen our lives. One primary way of doing so is to be well-versed in "the word of truth" (see 2 Timothy 2:15).

Let us seek to invest our lives, not merely spend our lives. Shopping and spending can be fun, but there is also a need for saving and investing. If we want to be prepared for emergencies, put our kids through college, and not be strapped financially in retirement, some saving and investing is in order. Likewise, in life, if spending and possessions are our "thing," we will typically be consumed and left with a narrow focus on items that have no ability to feed the soul or benefit anyone other than ourselves. Having nice things is fine when they occur in the natural flow of our lives, but emphasizing them leads to a self-centered, often frustrating existence. The advice of Jesus:

> Do not store up for yourselves treasures on earth, where moth and rust destroy, and where thieves break in and steal. But store up for yourselves treasures in heaven where moth and rust do not destroy, and where thieves do not break and steal. For where you treasure is, there your heart will be also (Matthew 6:19-21).

Let us seek to examine life, not merely absorb life. For this thought, these words definitely come to mind: "Dear friends, do not believe every spirit, but test the spirits to see whether they are from God, because many false prophets have gone out into the world" (1 John 4:1). We are bombarded every day with ideas and philosophies that vie for our attention and acceptance – "winning is everything" or (you have to love this one) "if you're not first you're last", "sexual practices are a matter of personal preference" (which basically translates to "nothing is off-limits or inappropriate"), or "get your piece of the pie" (meaning that your pursuits, your advantage, and your comfort and contentment come first, before anything else). If you watch TV, go to the movies, listen to contemporary music, read books, or go to work or most anywhere outside your home, you will be exposed to these and other ideas. The trick is to examine what circulates around us, in light of the mind of Christ, not merely absorb it. Otherwise, after hearing it over and over (which we will surely do) and thinking that tons of others have no problem with it so why should I, we end up wearing down and absorbing the questionable, the counter-productive, the unhealthy.

Let us seek to do what we're intended to do with life. Before we moved to San Diego, we loaded up the family one day and went off to see the Cincinnati Reds play in a major league baseball game. James was about kindergarten age at the time. As the game progressed, the Reds did some exciting things (this was in the era of "The Big Red Machine"). When one of the players hit a home run over the right field wall, I turned to our son and said, "James, did you see the home run?" Actually, he had missed it because he was eating his peanuts. Later, another player hit a long fly ball close to where we were sitting in left field. It would have been a home run but curved foul. I asked James, "Did you see the long fly?" No, he was watching all the activity on the scoreboard. Then, one of the Reds hit an inside the park home run, always an exciting play. As the player was racing around the bases, I tried to draw James' attention to what was happening on the field. He missed most of it because he was playing with his miniature souvenir bat. From a baseball purists' point of view, James wasn't doing what he was supposed to do at a ballgame. We were supposed to be watching the action of the game, but James was all caught up in other activities which, I guess for a five-year-old, is understandable.

When we think about life, however, our lives are so much more joyful and fulfilling when we seek to do what we are intended to do. And just what is it that we are intended to do? According to Matthew 6:33, we are intended to "seek first his kingdom and his righteousness." This won't exclude all "non-spiritual" activities from our lives, but it will keep us properly focused, deepening not merely expanding our lives, investing not merely spending our lives, examining not merely absorbing life. The result will be that our lives will be supported by and built upon the firmest foundation possible.

Another reason that accounts for joy in Christian living is this: *In the Christian life, we are strengthened by fellowship.* Among other things, the early Church devoted themselves faithfully to "fellowship" (see Acts 2:42). They were a community, sharing with one another, caring for one another, encouraging one another, supporting one another. They were tied to one another in a common cause, i.e., in negotiating the Christian life and the challenges of the world together, not on their own. They were, likewise, tied together in holding up Christ to the world. Ajith Fernando makes this interesting point: "According to the Bible the entire life, including spiritual growth, battling sin and Satan, and serving God, are intended to be done in community."[27]

Fellowship is still one of the great qualities of the Church and Christian living today. In contemporary America, isolation and feeling alone can be a real concern. Many families are scattered around the country. Neighbors are those who live in proximity but not necessarily folks that we interact with and know. Television, video games, and the internet keep many inside and occupied with these pursuits. The COVID-19 pandemic increased the intensity of these realities. Since we are social beings, our needs are not met by soap operas and hours spent on the internet. We need to feel loved,

---

27. Fernando, *Acts*, 125.

sense that we are known and not lost in the vast throng of humanity, and that someone will be concerned and available if life takes a turn down a rough road. This is the essence of fellowship in the Church.

Navy ships participate in an evolution that illustrates this thought very well. In order to stay steaming at sea, ships carry out what is called UNREP, or Underway Replenishment. If a ship needs to travel long distances or stay on station for an extended period of time, supply/auxiliary ships rendezvous with the ship to transfer food stores, parts, oil, or whatever else might be needed. The supply ship pulls up alongside the other ship while they both keep steaming at the same speed (at a safe but relatively close distance), lines or hoses are shot across, and the needed items are pumped or transferred from one to the other. Thus, the ship is able to continue on without pulling into port and losing vital time or compromising the mission.

Fellowship in the Church works the same way. As we steam through life, we pull up alongside one another and shoot across the lines of kindness, concern, and affection. Sometimes, we simply transfer friendship while sharing good times of interaction as we worship and serve Christ. At other times, we transfer our love and compassion, as well as the love and compassion of Christ, for grief, divorce, and the myriad of other personal and spiritual struggles that may arise in life. By so doing, in the strength of Christ, we hope to keep one another steaming over the seas of life without breaking down or having a serious interruption in our ability to keep sailing on. This strengthening fellowship is a great contributor to joy in our Christian lives.

Here's another reason why joy and the Christian life are inseparably linked: *In the Christian life, we are swept up in meaningful service and usefulness.* When we look around us today, "service" and "usefulness" are not always the bywords that we typically hear. We have touched on this before, but let's add a little more at this point. More often, the words that are prominent begin with the prefix "self" – self-interest, self-promotion, self-fulfillment. We do have to look after ourselves to a certain extent, but the "self" approach draws us inward so that things revolve around us, our feelings and desires. What results is disappointments are magnified, slights are duly noted and dwelt up until an opportunity comes to even the score, and "rights" are held onto and demanded so that we become difficult to be around. Most clear-thinking people would admit that this isn't a great way to live.

This is where service and usefulness come in. Helping, contributing, looking beyond ourselves gets out of those patterns of just defending and guarding our insulated, self-important world (which can be very exhausting, time consuming, and disastrous to relationships), and provides a sense that we are truly doing something good and worthwhile. These actions complete us as human beings as we become involved in the human experience beyond ourselves, reaching out and giving, not just taking and hoarding as we move through life.

Why should we believe in the importance and value of service and usefulness to others? Foremost, because to do so emulates Christ who "did not come to be served, but to serve, and to give his life as a ransom for many" (Matthew 20:28). Christ's joy did not come from the acclaim of the crowds or the ego satisfaction of having people hang on His words and marvel at what He could do. Instead, He found joy in useful service, in helping others have a better life here and opening up the prospect of a glorious eternity. We honor Him, continue His work, and demonstrate our gratitude by doing the same.

We also do the same because helping and serving others is a key indicator that we possess the mind and spirit of Christ and are making progress in seeking His will and not merely our own goals and pursuits. The Lord's face shines on those who assist the hungry, the thirsty, the stranger, those in need of clothing, the sick, and the imprisoned (see Matthew 25:31-46); not because a grand resume of good works will ease us into heaven on judgment day, but because many have come upon unfortunate circumstances in life and our concern holds up the love of Christ for difficult times and reveals our identification with Him.

And, we do the same simply because it lifts our spirits and makes us better people – people who refuse to allow the spirit of the age to have the upper hand and have been renewed in Christ. There is nothing quite like the sense of satisfaction and fulfillment that comes from making a difference for others on behalf of God and Christ.

Yet another reason why joy and Christian living team up so well is similar but still a little different from what we have just discussed: *In the Christian life, we are sustained by leaving a legacy.* After a certain age (maybe around forty or sometime thereafter), most of us begin to take stock of our lives and wonder what we have accomplished; have we done anything of lasting value. It's nice to have been here and, hopefully, we can recall a lot of rewarding moments and experiences but, when our earthly time is over, will anything live on because we did something of significance. During a time of depression in early 1841, Abraham Lincoln is reported to have said "that he would be 'more than willing to die' except 'that he had done nothing to make any human being remember that he had lived.'"[28] That would change for Lincoln, but a lot of us begin to wonder during the second half of life if the same applies to us.

The reality is that not many of us will be included in history books for being President of the United States, for great feats of heroism, or for transforming society in some wonderful way. After realizing this, we can still leave an outstanding legacy that continues long after we are gone. It

28. James M. McPherson, *This Mighty Scourge: Perspectives on the Civil War* (New York: Oxford University Press, 2007), 193.

might relate to the investment we make in our children and grandchildren, enriching and guiding their lives so that future generations benefit from what we passed on. It might relate to other youth that we have taught in Sunday school or mentored in youth groups or some other setting. It might relate to those that we encouraged or somehow assisted in a time of need, enabling them to press on with their families and other responsibilities. Certainly, it can be related to those who we have nurtured in Christ, pointing them in the direction of the abundant life that comes through Him, both for the present and for eternity.

Often we do not know the impact that we have had. I remember returning to visit the first full-time church where Judy and I ministered. I had helped one of the faithful members through the demanding time of the death of her husband. Now, years later, she shared that a verse I relayed at the time had meant so much and had helped her over the years – "But those who hope in the LORD will renew their strength. They will soar on wings like eagles; they will run and not grow weary, they will walk and not be faint" (Isaiah 40:31 – we referred to this verse in Chapter Eight). I had mentioned to her that this was not a time for soaring like an eagle or for running and not growing weary, but in the Lord it was still possible to walk and not faint. It meant more than I ever knew until then.

I also encountered a couple during that visit that I had known during my years at the church. Their first attempt at having children resulted, unfortunately, in a stillbirth. They did not attend the church where I was ministering, but their pastor was on vacation and I was called to the hospital to help with pastoral care. I might have made a follow-up call but, basically, I didn't have contact with them again until this visit several years later. The husband wanted me to know that they truly appreciated the support I had provided at the time, that they had been able to manage the extreme disappointment in the strength of the Lord, and that they had been able to have other children since. In representing the Lord, I had been able to contribute something of lasting value.

We may not be a minister in the sense that we earn part or all of our income by serving a congregation or another arm of the Lord's work in some capacity, but we are all ministers in the vineyard of Christ. All of us can impact the lives of others, enriching them and helping to prepare them for eternity. As we do, we are sustained with the realization that we are leaving a legacy that will continue on even after we have gone to be with the Lord.

Finally, let us remember this about joy and Christian living: *In the Christian life, we are surrounded by hope.* In the trenches of life, hope is often what keeps us going. Generally, hope is the idea that, in the midst of trials and struggles, things will work out. It is the expectation that things will get better or that what we desire will come to pass. With God, it is the anticipation that His promises of strength and patience to see things through and overcome will be fulfilled. With God, it is the trust that a better world awaits those who love and live in Him. In Titus 1:2, Paul wrote about our faith and knowledge that rests "on the hope of eternal life, which God, who does not lie, promised before the beginning of time."

While serving as a chaplain, I conducted numerous training sessions on the subject of *suicide prevention*, looking at such things as factors that lead to suicidal thoughts or an actual attempt, warning signs, and actions to take when suicidal thoughts are suspected. As you perhaps know, one of the factors involved is that individuals begin to feel that the problems are insurmountable, that there is very little if any hope, and there is nothing to look forward to, only more difficulties. Intervention seeks to help the person see the issues in a different light (for instance, that the problems are temporary and that there are resources available to aid in dealing with the matters at hand) and restore a measure of hope.

Spiritual resources, specifically the friendship of Christ, head the list of available means of assistance and support. In Christ, it is always too soon to despair. In Christ, we always have something to look forward to, viz., His presence, help, concern, and ultimately His coming again. Consider the following:

When life is good and moving along smoothly, we look forward to Christ.

When life is not so good and not moving along so smoothly, we look forward to Christ.

When praises come our way, we look forward to Christ.

When criticism or disappointments mount, we look forward to Christ.

When friends are true and reliable, we look forward to Christ.

When friends misunderstand, say things that are false and go off in a huff, we look forward to Christ.

When we feel loved and accepted, we look forward to Christ.

When we feel alone, we look forward to Christ.

When health greets us in the morning, we look forward to Christ.

When illness strikes, we look forward to Christ.

When work is rewarding and enjoyable, we look forward to Christ.

When work is demanding and not so enjoyable, we look forward to Christ.

When life gives us its best, we look forward to Christ.

When life tumbles in, we look forward to Christ.

When we are in the prime of life, we look forward to Christ.

When death knocks on our door, we look forward to Christ.

The third verse of the marvelous hymn, "Great is Thy Faithfulness," reminds us that, in Christ, we have "strength for today and bright hope for tomorrow":

> Pardon for sin and a peace that endureth,
> Thine own dear presence to cheer and to guide,
> Strength for today and bright hope for tomorrow -
> Blessings all mine, with ten thousand beside.

Indeed, "bright hope" in the promises and faithfulness of God and Christ as we look forward to His return and the glory of a better place is just one more reason that leads to joy in Christian living.

Supported by a Firm Foundation/Strengthened by Fellowship/Swept-Up in Meaningful Service and Usefulness/Sustained by Leaving a Legacy/Surrounded by Hope. All of these facets of Christian living are possible and real because of the umbrella that stretches over them all – *we are with Christ.* In Him and in living for Him, there is, without question, overwhelming and ultimate joy.

THE JOY OF HOME AND HEAVEN

"We are confident, I say, and would prefer to be
away from the body and at home with the Lord.
So we make it our goal to please him, whether
we are at home in the body or away from it."

2 Corinthians 5:8-9

"... but rejoice that your names are written in heaven."

Luke 10:20b

One of the most famous quotes about "home" is the one by John Howard
Payne – "Mid pleasures and palaces though we may roam, Be it ever so
humble, there's no place like home." Home, indeed, has a special place in
our hearts and, as Ann Douglas has stated, it is "an invention on which no
one has yet improved."

The thought/theme of "home" crops up all around us in inspirational
sayings, music, art, literature, and in just our own musings. Here are a couple
of other quotations that relay some interesting thoughts about "home":

"Life is a voyage that's homeward bound." – Herman
Melville

"A child on a farm sees a plane fly overhead and dreams of a faraway place. A traveler on the plane sees the farmhouse and dreams of home." – Carl Burns

"Having a place to go – is a home. Having someone to love – is a family. Having both – is a blessing." – Donna Hedges

"The best way to keep children at home is to make the home atmosphere pleasant, and let the air out of the tires." – Dorothy Parker

"Having someone wonder where you are when you don't come home at night is a very old human need." - Margaret Mead

"A person travels the world over in search of what he needs and returns home to find it." – George Moore

"Home is the place where, when you have to go there, they have to take you in." – Robert Frost

The truth is that we yearn for home, thoughts of home cheer us and keep us going, home is a sanctuary and place of rest, home draws us back to its warm environs no matter where in the world we have traveled and no matter what we have become in our adult lives.[29] Vocabulary words that center around "home" emphasize these realities. Words such as "homecoming," "hometown," "homemade" (e.g., pies, breads, and soups), and "homegrown" usually bring a smile and put us in a favorable frame of mind. As Lewis Grizzard has said, "It's difficult to think anything but pleasant thoughts while eating a homegrown tomato."

---

29. I realize that these thoughts are not true for everyone. All homes are not what they are intended to be and do not conjure up warm and hospitable feelings. Where this is the case, I trust that the thought of having a home with God is very meaningful.

When Jan Karon began her books in *The Mitford Series*, she invited us to a cozy, comfortable experience by entitling the first volume, *At Home in Mitford*. Likewise, the first volume in the second series about her now retired, fictional small-town minister is entitled, *Home to Holly Springs*. Every Memorial Day weekend, thousands get all choked up when they sing "(Back Home Again in) Indiana" at the Indianapolis 500. I was watching the movie "Forrest Gump" the other night. You may recall that Forrest goes on a three-year running jag, back and forth across America. When asked "why," he merely says that he got it in his mind to run. Later on, he says that perhaps part of it was to deal with the past so he could move forward. After all this running, he suddenly stops in the middle of a remote highway, turns to those who are following him, and says that he is tired. Where does he want to go now? You guessed it – home.

Several music artists have songs about being on the road and traveling all around the world (note Michael Buble's and Blake Shelton's "Home" and Bon Jovi's "Who Says You Can't Go Home"); now, there's only one place they want to go – home. We may be in some glamour spot such as Paris, some spot rich in history such as Rome, some spot steeped in beauty and awe such as the Grand Canyon, but the time eventually comes when we say, "This has all been great, but I'm ready to go home now." Many agree there's nothing like sleeping in your own bed, at home.

Why is this? The reasons vary but, for a lot of us, home represents the place of security and youthful innocence we knew before all of the responsibilities of adulthood set in. Home conjures up images of acceptance, belonging, understanding, unconditional love, concern, support, and the freedom to be ourselves. Home reminds us of a less complicated, carefree time when Little League and soccer dominated our thoughts and when parents, teachers, coaches, ministers, and others were true heroes. With encouragement from those who believe in us, home is a place to become what we are capable of and what we desire. And, as the quotations above indicate, home may be the fallback, the retreat where we can go when other options dry up or where our absence is noted with uneasiness if we are late in coming home. Without question, home is one of the strongest images that keeps coming back and intruding into our thoughts as we live out this earthly life. In the process, it conveys a lot of joy.

Of course, our interest here is with the spiritual concept of "home," and this is a powerful image with many of the same features as well. When we think of our spiritual home, our minds focus on the love, understanding, acceptance, and support of our heavenly Parent, of Christ, and the Holy Spirit. Just as the shepherd went out to find the one lost sheep when ninety-nine were in the fold (Luke 15:3-7), our spiritual home centers around God's concern and compassion. Being at home with God empowers us to become what we are capable of and intended to be, i.e., His children with overcoming strength and power for the living of life. And, when the world turns cold, when our way travels uphill and requires more effort than normal, and prospects grow dim, our spiritual home is a place of refuge and rest.

There are many scriptural accounts that involve home. Adam and Eve are driven out of their home in the Garden of Eden after their act of disobedience. Abram (later Abraham) sets out to the land that God promises as an inheritance, leaving home and all that is familiar. Joseph is sold into slavery by his brothers and travels to Egypt, forcefully removed from home and his father. Ruth leaves her homeland to go with Naomi to Bethlehem. David travels from home to play the harp for Saul and to bring a "care package" from home to his brothers in the army, which leads to remarkable developments in his life. God's people are carried away from home to captivity in Assyria and Babylon. The Prodigal Son leaves home for adventure and excitement, only to return when the ways of the world prove to be cold and empty. All of these accounts contain valuable spiritual lessons, but the one that best combines the two aspects of our spiritual home (i.e., both present and eternal dimensions) is the Christmas account. Why? Because the Christmas narrative is about Mary and Joseph going home, so Jesus can leave home, becoming one like us in order to provide us with a home here that will, eventually, result in an eternal home. Let us not forget that we are intended to be at home with God now (with all of the good images that this implies) as we prepare to be at home with Him forever. The events surrounding the birth of Christ bring all of this into focus.

You may not be reading this at Christmas time, but the Christmas account truly informs us about the biblical concept of "home." Therefore, let us glean what we can from its wonderful message about God, Christ, and our spiritual home.

Ideas of getting home, being home, and/or thinking of home underlie the first Christmas and our observance of it still today. Then, Mary and Joseph went home to Bethlehem to register for the census. Today, have you noticed that a great many of the songs of Christmas emphasize this theme of going home? Numerous artists have recorded such seasonal favorites as "(There's No Place Like) Home for the Holidays," "There's No Christmas Like a Home Christmas," and, of course, "I'll Be Home for Christmas." The latter song is perhaps the one most beloved by service men and women, yearning to make it home "if only in my dreams." These are just a few of the songs that talk about the physical side of being home for Christmas.

However, the true message of Christmas centers on being home spiritually. This is why Jesus came – to provide us with a spiritual home and to lead us there. The message of the Bible is that we need a spiritual home and that it is available to us, that we need Christ to help us get there, and that, on our own, we are away from our true roots and our true home.

This reality is forced upon us when we call to mind such passages as Isaiah 53:6a, "We all, like sheep, have gone astray, each of us has turned to his own way . . .". Romans 3:23 reminds us "for all have sinned and fall short of the glory of God," meaning that we have lived apart from the Lord. Ephesians 2 talks about the fact that we have too often "followed the ways of this world" (vs. 2), "but now in Christ Jesus you who once were far away have been brought near through the blood of Christ" (vs. 13). Another way to say this is that Christ has brought us home. And the whole image of the Prodigal Son is about our need to return home to the Father, because home with Him is where we truly belong. The world apart from God never truly satisfies. Having been created and given life by God, we are intended to "live and move and have our being" in Him (Acts 17:28).

In his book, *Can I Know God*, the great English preacher and author of the last century, W. E. Sangster, includes a sermon entitled, "The Homesickness of the Soul." On this thought of not being satisfied with the things of earth, Sangster writes:

> I warn you against supposing that if only you had more of this or more of that, you would be completely satisfied. It is an illusion. Earth cannot satisfy you. William Watson – in his poem "World-Strangeness – asked:
>
> > In this house with starry dome,
> > Floored with gemlike plains and seas,
> > Shall I never feel at home,
> > Never wholly be at ease?
>
> Never! You weren't meant to.[30]

I think it is unfair to merely dismiss this world or look at it with disdain as some tend to do. God created it with beauty, with all necessary resources, with the possibility of providing us with many uplifting experiences and relationships, and with the prospect of having us contribute in many

---

30. Sangster, *Can I Know God*, 56.

worthwhile, rewarding ways. However, God's people realize that it is a temporary place that was never intended to be the totality of our existence. As the old chorus emphasizes, "This world is not my home, I'm just a-passing through." Being temporary, it was never intended to satisfy us on all fronts. That happens only in being at home with God.

Sangster goes on to describe two men in his sermon. The first man gave up on the faith of his youth and, having tasted what the non-spiritual world had to offer, concluded that he needed nothing more. Sangster remarks, "He had not only lost his way; he had lost his address."[31] In short, there is a place where we belong and when we move away from that place (i.e., from God), we have lost the address of our true residence.

The second person was a man who, for many years, was locked in combat between his better self and the deadly craving for strong drink. Often this man would come to Sangster, and they would go into the chapel to pray. One afternoon, as they were praying, the man broke down completely and began to cry uncontrollably. He blurted out, "I know I'm in the gutter. I know it. But Oh! . . . I don't belong there, do I? Tell me, I don't belong there . . .". Sangster put his arm around the man and said, "No, you don't belong there; you belong to God."[32] Like many, the man had lost his way. He had strayed from home, but he still knew where he belonged. He still knew that his true address was at home, with God.

What all of this means is that we are intended to live at home with God in this life, and, praise God, we have an eternal home with Him when this life is over. This is what Paul was referring to in our opening verses (2 Cor. 5:8-9) when he talked about being "away from the body and at home with the Lord." Jesus, Himself, reassured us when He said, "In my Father's house are many rooms; if it were not so, I would have told you. I am going there to

---

31. Ibid., 59.
32. Ibid., 61.

prepare a place for you. And if I go and prepare a place for you, I will come back and take you to be with me that you also may be where I am" (John 14:2-3). Quite simply, we have a spiritual home and a place to be now, and we have a spiritual home and a place to be forever.

What does our eternal, spiritual home look like? Most of us are probably familiar with the images of heaven that primarily come to us from the book of Revelation. It is a place of great glory, splendor, and beauty as seen in Revelation 21:19-21. Heaven, our eternal home, also has these wonderful and astonishing features:

Disappointments and Worries are Never Experienced – Rev. 21:4a reveals that God will wipe away every tear from our eyes. The tear-producing struggles and anxious moments that we know here are nonexistent in heaven.

Fellowship and Relationships are Never Interrupted – Rev. 21:4b reminds us that "there will be no more death or mourning . . .". No more parting with loved ones and no more painful goodbyes and spending months apart for deployments and other operations as our military members often experience. Separations are nonexistent in heaven.

Dangers are Never a Factor – Rev. 21:4b also points out that pain will never surface in our eternal home. Pain-producing possibilities such as life-threatening illnesses, unexpected accidents, or personal attacks are nonexistent in heaven.

Additionally, *Needs are Forever Met* – Rev. 7:16-17a states that those around the throne will never again experience hunger or thirst, "For the Lamb at the center of the throne will be their shepherd; he will lead them to springs of living water." Likewise, "the city does not need the sun or the moon to shine on it, for the glory of God gives it light, and the Lamb is its lamp" (Rev. 21:23). Stressing out about needs is nonexistent in heaven.

Sin and Evil are Forever Vanquished – "Nothing impure will ever enter it [the new Jerusalem], nor will anyone who does what is shameful or deceitful, but only those whose names are written in the Lamb's book of life" (Rev. 21:27). The crippling power of Satan that we have struggled with and often succumbed to in this life is nonexistent in heaven.

And, *Our Joy is Forever Complete* – In Revelation 19:6-7, we find the redeemed shouting, "Hallelujah! For our Lord God Almighty reigns. Let us rejoice and be glad and give him glory! For the wedding of the Lamb has come, and his bride has made herself ready." Then, the angel said: "Write: 'Blessed are those who are invited to the wedding supper of the Lamb'" (Rev. 19:9). Anything that would interfere with our joy is nonexistent in heaven. Eternal blessedness and joy are the earmarks of those in heaven because "Now the dwelling of God is with men, and he will live with them. They will be his people, and God himself will be with them and be their God" (Rev. 21:3). In our heavenly home, there is uninterrupted joy, forever.

This is all set in motion with Jesus leaving home and coming to earth to be our Savior. Of course, the path runs through His earthly life, His ministry, His crucifixion and death on the cross, His time in the grave, His resurrection, and His ascension and reception back with the Father. The details of this plan actually begin in the book of Genesis where God already has it in mind to bring us home to Him. However, the execution of the plan begins in Bethlehem, with Mary and Joseph going home, so Jesus can leave home, to come and make possible both our present and our eternal home with God and Himself. And what a home it is, for "No eye has seen, no ear has heard, no mind has conceived what God has prepared for those who love him" (1 Cor. 2:9). Being at home with God brings incredible, indescribable joy.

In concluding this chapter, another Christmas song about "home" comes to mind – "Hurry Home for Christmas." It, too, has been recorded by a number of artists and talks about scurrying home for Christmas so that jingle bells can jingle and so there will be cheer all around. It closes with the admonition, "Don't stop until you get here."

Again, it may or may not be the Christmas season as you read this, but the spiritual message is still the same – hurry home to Christ, to the Christ of Christmas and the manger, to the Christ of Calvary and the empty tomb, for He came to reunite us with the Father and to make it possible for us to live and dwell with Him. This is our true address. This is where we truly belong, where we are truly wanted, where we will truly experience life to its fullest and live eternally with God. Yes, "hurry home for Christmas" or for whatever time of year it happens to be. That is, hurry home to God and to Christ who are waiting to receive you with open arms and welcome you into eternal fellowship with them. Yes, hurry home to God and Christ, don't stop until you get there. I repeat, hurry home, don't stop until you get there.

EPILOGUE

"I delight greatly in the LORD; my soul rejoices in my God.
For he has clothed me with garments of salvation
and arrayed me in a robe of righteousness . . .".

Isaiah 61:10a

"Rejoice in the Lord always. I will say it again: Rejoice!"

Philippians 4:4

During my first year after retiring from the Navy, I taught a course on World Religions for one of our state universities in Connecticut. The first time that I taught the course was at one of their extension centers that happened to be an hour away from where we lived. Since the class was scheduled in the evening and lasted three hours, it was way past sunset each time I jumped in the car to go home. Driving up, I always stopped at the main campus to check my mailbox, etc. Driving home, I took a route that was a little shorter than going back to the town where the university is located. This "shortcut" was over roads that I had never driven before and, thus, every time I traveled this new and unfamiliar section was in the dark.

As the semester progressed, I wanted to show Judy the university campus (about twenty-five miles away) as well as the extension center where I was teaching. We had a nice Sunday drive going to both locations, then took the route home that I had only seen in the dark before.

It truly was an "eye-opening" experience to finally see things in the light of day. At one point, off to the right, there was a beautiful lake that I had never seen. I knew it had to be there somewhere since I always saw the sign for "Lake Road" as I wandered home. It was a wonderful view that I had missed in all of my other trips. As we continued, there were several nice homes and housing developments along the way, and a couple of scenic vistas that, of course, I had missed in the dark. I noticed several buildings and businesses that I was not aware of in my previous travels. It turns out that there was even a Hypnosis Center just off one of the state highways that I was using. Now, if I ever want to be hypnotized, I know where to go.

As you have made this trip along the road of "joy," I hope that you have become aware of things that you didn't know prior to the trip. As I have tried to emphasize, fullness of joy is found only in God and does not depend on favorable circumstances always occurring in order to be experienced. Certainly, none of us are able to completely avoid unfavorable circumstances, but joy does not have to desert us just because everything is not moving in the direction that we prefer. The "confidence in our ability, through Him, to ultimately triumph and overcome in life" that we discussed at the very beginning never leaves us when we commit our lives to the Lord and live in His glorious presence.

The verses that begin these final thoughts are very interesting. Since we have so much to be thankful for and joyful about, the apostle Paul encourages us to always be in a state of rejoicing. As we ponder this admonition, we need to keep in mind the situation of the one who was encouraging such a sweeping idea. As Paul writes to the Philippians, he is "in chains for Christ" (1:13), confined in prison. In spite of this, there is no *bickering* or complaining, just the thought of rejoicing in Christ. Over the course of his travels and labors for the Lord, Paul experienced a great number of hardships and a great amount of opposition and persecution (see 2 Corinthians 11:21-28). In spite of this, there is no *bitterness*, just the thought of rejoicing in Christ. And, there are things in his life that he is not proud of, viz., his previous opposition to the faith and his prior harassment of Christians, even consenting to their death (see Acts 7:24-8:1). Discarding any self-condemnation, there is no *brooding*, just the thought of rejoicing in Christ.

The secret as to how Paul is able to do this and the key to us following in his footsteps is that his rejoicing and ours is always "in the Lord." As we noted earlier, there will be times when we are experiencing "general" joy, as good things are taking place. However, biblical/spiritual joy is never limited to these times alone. With God, Christ, and the Holy Spirit always working on our behalf, our lives are always dialed in to "overcome." Isaiah 64:4 provides a wonderful thought along these lines: "Since ancient times no one has heard, no ear has perceived, no eye has seen any God besides you, who acts on behalf of those who wait for him."

Another proof of this reality is that, when we have this rejoicing attitude and refuse to be anxious by turning things over to God, His peace "which transcends all understanding, will guard your hearts and your minds in Christ Jesus" (Phil. 4:4-7). God's peace for managing whatever comes in life is incomprehensible. It makes no sense why God's people are able to press on through the most trying conflicts and burdens. Don't try to understand it or figure it out, just rejoice that this peace is real and that, as we already observed, we can truly "do everything through him who gives me strength" (Phil. 4:13).

The Isaiah passage above reminds us of another reason why we are constantly able to rejoice. God has clothed us "with garments of salvation" and arrayed us "in a robe of righteousness." This is now fully realized with the coming of our Lord and Savior Jesus Christ and what His death, burial, and resurrection accomplished for us all. Life can, indeed, be taxing and demanding at times; we should never gloss over this reality. But, in the end, this need not take away our joy, for God and Christ and the Holy Spirit are always present to sustain, comfort, strengthen, forgive, and guide us. They are always present to remind us of our life in Christ and our eternal home. This is why we are able to "rejoice in the Lord always."

Allow me to wrap everything up with the following two thoughts. Not too long ago, Judy and I participated in our annual ritual of picking strawberries. We love fresh strawberries and so we eat some and put them on ice cream, and Judy freezes some so we have them through the winter and she makes others into milk shakes, jam, and desserts. After picking a good amount, we went into The Country Store to pay for them, where they have an array of other goods as well. In one corner of the store was an assortment of coffee mugs. The mugs had various sayings about Friendship and Kindness, and even some mugs inscribed with "Amazing Grace" and "Faith, Hope, and Love." However, as you might suspect, the one that caught my eye was the mug that said, "Choose Joy." After our journey together, I trust that all of us will follow through and "Choose Joy," so that we can live the life that God has in mind for us all.

And then there is this. Perhaps you heard about the utility company that sent an unusual notice to one of its customers who was long overdue in paying his bill. The notice read: "We would be delighted if you would pay your bill promptly. If not, you will probably be de-lighted." I pray that we will not allow the challenges and circumstances that rise up in life to "de-light" us, i.e., to rob us of the joy, delight, and gladness of our faith. In the Lord, there is full, complete, and ultimate joy that nothing can remove or destroy and that, I believe, we are intended to experience on some level each day that we live. May God bless each one of us as we live in His wonderful, overwhelming joy and as we prepare for that eternal joy that will never end.